how would would buddha think?

1,501 Right-Intention Teachings
for Cultivating a Peaceful Mind

• • •

BARBARA ANN KIPFER, PhD

New Harbinger Publications, Inc.

Publisher's Note

This publication is designed to provide accurate and authoritative informa-tion in regard to the subject matter covered. It is sold with the understanding that the publisher is not engaged in rendering psychological, financial, legal, or other professional services. If expert assistance or counseling is needed, the services of a competent professional should be sought.

Distributed in Canada by Raincoast Books

Copyright © 2016 by Barbara Ann Kipfer
New Harbinger Publications, Inc.
5674 Shattuck Avenue
Oakland, CA 94609
www.newharbinger.com

Cover design by Debbie Berne; Text design by Michele Waters-Kermes; Acquired by Melissa Valentine; Edited by Ken Knabb

Library of Congress Cataloging-in-Publication Data

Names: Kipfer, Barbara Ann, author.
Title: How would Buddha think? : 1,501 right-intention teachings for
   cultivating a peaceful mind / Barbara Ann Kipfer, PhD.
Description: Oakland, CA : New Harbinger Publications, Inc., 2016.
   | Series: The new harbinger following Buddha series
Identifiers: LCCN 2016001940 (print) | LCCN 2016013112 (ebook) |
   ISBN 9781626253155 (pbk. : alk. paper) | ISBN 9781626253162
   (pdf e-book) | ISBN 9781626253179 (epub) | ISBN 9781626253162
   (PDF e-book) | ISBN 9781626253179 (ePub)
Subjects: LCSH: Eightfold Path. | Religious life--Buddhism. |
   Peace--Religious aspects--Buddhism.
Classification: LCC BQ4320 .K57 2016 (print) | LCC BQ4320
   (ebook) | DDC 294.3/42--dc23
LC record available at http://lccn.loc.gov/2016001940

18   17   16   10 9 8 7 6 5 4 3 2 1
First Printing

Thank you to New Harbinger for the opportunity to present this material. A big giant thanks to my husband, Paul Magoulas, and my sons, Kyle Kipfer and Keir Magoulas. They are a big inspiration for me on the Noble Eightfold Path.

—Barbara Ann Kipfer

Contents

Introduction

The Buddha said, "All that we are is the result of what we have thought." Each word and every action begins with a thought. With thought coming first, before the times when you are kind or unkind, helpful or harmful in speech or action, the precept of Right Intention is something each of us needs to understand deeply and learn to work with.

This book explains how you are not your thoughts, but also how you are what you think. It sounds contradictory, but it is actually complementary.

We pretty much believe the things we say inside our heads, the "stories" we tell ourselves. Imaginary conversations and imaginary events continually take place in the mind. This book reminds you that thoughts and stories are invented and you do not need to believe them or think they represent truth. That is what is meant by "you are not your thoughts."

However, do you think that things that go on in your mind do not affect your world and that of others? The Buddha's quote, above, implies that every thought is part of karma. Karma is not just about you and the present; it is about all interconnected beings in the past, present, and future. Anything that happens in life starts with a thought.

So the precept of Right Intention in the Noble Eightfold Path sets out to rectify wrong intention governed by desire, wrong intention created by ill will, and wrong intention caused by harmful thought. A person leaning toward taking a job because the higher salary will allow him or her to buy a fancy car or more clothes is using wrong intention because this desire is materialistic in nature. If a person wishes someone was not around anymore, that is also wrong intention because it is actually wishing harm to someone. Any harmful or unskillful thought is wrong intention.

Notice that in these examples, the person has not yet communicated or taken action. The thoughts are taking place in the mind and only that person has been privy to them. However, this indicates that the person is feeling desire, greed, craving, clinging, ill will, and other negative emotions. Karma says that "you don't get away with anything," meaning that these harmful thoughts have harmful consequences, direct and indirect, now and in the future. Negative thoughts have bad effects, just like negative speech and negative actions.

The mind's intentions form a crucial link to our speech and actions. Actions and speech always point back to the thoughts from which they came. Thought is the forerunner of action and speech, stirring them into activity, using them as its instruments for expressing its aims and ideals. These aims and ideals, our intentions, in turn point back a further step, to our views and values. When wrong views and values prevail, the outcome is wrong intention, giving rise to unwholesome actions and speech.

So, when people set out to gain wealth, position, and power without regard for consequences, the cause for the endless competition, conflict, injustice, and oppression does not lie outside the mind. These are all manifestations of intentions, outcroppings of thoughts driven by greed, by hatred, by delusion. But when right intentions are behind your thoughts, the actions and speech produced will be right. The law of karma says that all actions bring consequences, including thoughts.

In cultivating renunciation, the real issue is not renouncing objects or possessions themselves, but renouncing your attachment to them. In cultivating goodwill and loving-kindness, the issue is not that you don't do it at all, but that you, like most of us, probably only rarely cultivate goodwill and loving-kindness for all beings without discrimination. By cultivating nonharming, you grow your compassion.

The focus of *How Would Buddha Think?* is training yourself to understand that thoughts govern every word and deed. If you think loving, compassionate thoughts—creating the intention of doing no harm and of refraining from unskillful actions and words—you are taking a step on the Buddha's path.

How Would Buddha Think? helps you learn to watch the countless thoughts and to discover perceptions and states of consciousness in an effort to develop calm and peace in your mind, and therefore in your life. The purpose of this book is to teach and remind, so that you become kinder in your thoughts. This is a book for cultivating awareness in the area of Right Intention. It is about abandoning wrong and harmful thought and "doing no harm."

If you wrote down everything you think about, you would see that a very large percentage of it is rehashing or remembering the past or planning, anticipating, or worrying about the future. That means that you are not experiencing life to the fullest. You are adding in your judgments, your likes and dislikes and other opinions, rather than seeing and experiencing what is real and true. The teachings and essays in this book point not just to your harmful thoughts, but also to the good intentions you have and how to pay attention to and cultivate those thoughts.

The book has three parts: the teachings in list form that can be used to become more awake and aware during everyday life, a series of short essays about topics pertaining to Right Intention, and some meditations focused on this part of the Noble Eightfold Path.

Spending a few minutes each day to read an essay or selecting a teaching to write on a sticky note or share with others will create a practice of mindfulness in which you cultivate Right Intention and Right Thought. Your practice will help bring happiness to yourself and to others. My wish is that, along with your speech and actions, you will find yourself becoming more awake and aware as to your mind's intentions and what effect your thoughts will have.

Teachings

- Make believe that your inner voice has a body of its own. Imagine it as a person talking to you from the outside, saying everything that your inner voice would say. Do this for a day. The same nonstop talk that used to be inside is now sitting there with you. Externalizing the voice like this is the best way to gain awareness of what you live with on the inside.

- Your visions will become clear only when you can look into your own heart. One who looks outside is dreaming. One who looks inside may awaken.

- Close your eyes and stay alert. Watch the mind respond to stimuli—sounds outside, thoughts and feelings inside—and see how noticing them restores the mind's balance.

- Even if you turn off the TV when eating, the TV in your mind is still on. So you also have to stop the TV—the conversation and images—in your head.

- The mind is clear except when clouded by defilements such as delusion. Delusion comes in three forms: attachment, aversion, and ignorance.

- Be alert to the tendency of the mind to busy itself, to look around for things to watch or think about. This is just a habit. Each time you notice it you lessen the tendency for it to happen again.

- What is vital is not thinking about the present, but actually being that present moment.

- Gazillions of things are going on in the world. You can think about it all you want, but most of life is going to keep on happening without your thoughts being involved.

- Don't allow your thoughts to have power over you. Acknowledge that thoughts are not facts. You can shape your world through the wisdom of mindful awareness and insight.

- Be determined not to kill, not to let others kill, and not to condone any act of killing in the world, even in your thinking.

- Being precise in your awareness helps to tease apart the tangling of thoughts and feelings and to dispel the illusion of their solidness.

- Sometimes the best way to be in touch with your feelings or thoughts is to stop feeling and stop thinking for a moment. Give yourself the gift of silence. Give space to your feelings and thoughts.

- Insight meditation practice is bringing your awareness to whatever arises and focusing firmly on it. Deepen the focus and analyze the thoughts and feelings, but be careful not to identify with them.

- Recognize that even the strongest emotions are temporary. They have power over a person for only as long as that person gives power to them.

- You don't need to know all the answers. Learn what you think you'd benefit from knowing.

- Describing to yourself the character of your own thoughts, and even attaching a simplistic, self-deprecating label to them, can help you to avoid taking yourself too seriously.

- By constantly observing your thoughts, you disengage yourself from the tendency to allow untoward thoughts to grow into evil intentions.

- Develop a mind that clings to nothing. Thoughts arise, sensations are felt, the senses are open and receiving, there are preferences and opinions—arising and then departing. Those thoughts cloud the truth of the present moment.

- If someone speaks or acts with pure thought, happiness follows that person like a shadow that never leaves.

- Memories, plans, feelings, and thoughts are fine—but attaching to them, obsessing over them, and letting them rule you causes suffering.

- Recognize an emotion (such as anger) at the moment it forms, understanding that it is but a thought and allowing it to dissipate spontaneously. This will help you avoid the chain reaction it could unleash.

- How you act and think creates new habits and conditions for how you will act and think in the future.

- What matters is whether you are aware of your thoughts and feelings during meditation. Your thoughts are just thoughts—they are not you or reality.

- According to the Buddha's teachings, the most basic condition for happiness is freedom from anger, despair, jealousy, and delusion.

- Experiencing angry thoughts does not make you an angry person, as long as you don't hold on to those angry thoughts but simply let them pass through your mind.

- Remind yourself how fulfilled you already are and you'll have an easier perspective about all the stuff you think you want. You'll see how much you really don't need it.

- When you simplify your communications by eliminating the irrelevant, you infuse what you do communicate with greater importance, dignity, and intention.

- Whenever you can find time for just being, drop all doing. Thinking is doing, concentration is doing, and contemplation is doing.

- If a thought arises, just look at the nature of that thought itself; this will cause the thought to lose its power and dissolve of its own accord.

- When you see that you don't need to pay any attention to your thoughts, it becomes easier to drop them.

- You can be mindful in the bath or shower, watch your breath in bed before sleeping, and analyze your thoughts while walking through the shopping mall.

- You aren't in charge of your life, no one can be, and you cannot control what other people think of you.

- Hell is created by your thoughts, and so is heaven.

- Make good friends with your habitual patterns of thinking by accepting these repetitive thoughts. If you stop feeling guilty about them, they will lose much of their power over you.

- Have the humility to mindfully and accurately assess your intentions and motivations, your strengths and weaknesses, so that you can recognize your spiritual interrelatedness with other beings.

- The mental voice within you is never content and always has a problem with something. You will never be free of problems until you are free from the mental voice and from unskillful thought.

- Do just one thing at a time, keeping your mind in the present. Practice doing it slower, with more intention, and more awareness and respect.

- Original big mind is mind before thinking shatters it into a billion ideas and preferences. It is a pure open space without attractions or aversions. It is pure essence, direct experience.

- Peace of mind produces right values,
  right values produce right thoughts,
  right thoughts produce right actions.

- You can often balance hatred or anger
  by developing thoughts of compassion
  and forgiveness.

- If a behavior or way of thinking does not
  have a positive payoff of making your life
  happy, it can and should be changed.

- Because practice enlarges your perspective
  beyond identifying with thoughts and
  opinions, it helps you have more patience
  and tolerance.

- Do not automatically echo another person's
  general grumble. Take the time to think
  through your opinions and respond
  sincerely, if at all. A well-judged silence
  might be best.

- Freedom from craving is an important practice. Look deeply into the nature of what you think will bring you happiness and consider whether it may, in fact, cause others to suffer.

- Tiredness is the product of a day filled with wasted thought, with feelings of anxiety and worry, anger and resentment. These negative mental states do more to sap energy than anything else.

- If kindness, generosity, love, and wisdom motivate your intentions, happiness will follow.

- Admire from the depths of the heart your own virtues. Take joy in the good things you have done in this and previous lives, thinking: *I really did something good!*

- Think of the center of your being as the center of a cyclone or tornado. Whatever happens around it does not affect it. It is eternal silence and calm.

- Nothing contributes so much to tranquilize the mind as a steady purpose outside oneself.

- Think about what it means to take a vow of silence for a short period of time, a personal time of rest. This would be a silence that is not broken by mental chatter or interpersonal exchanges.

- Your thoughts are part of your karma. Your likes and dislikes, opinions, concepts— which drive you from action to action— create more karma. What kind of karma are your thoughts creating?

- Begin a meditation by paying attention to your thoughts. Notice what the voices inside your head are telling you. Are the thoughts positive or negative? How do they make you feel?

- Repeated good intentions can generate a powerful inner voice that will keep you on track.

- Think good and generous thoughts. As you think, so shall you become. Your thoughts and feelings go into everything you build, cook, create, give, and say.

- Your worst enemy cannot harm you as much as your own thoughts.

- Think about what friendship means to you and what you value most in a friend. Think about what you would like to offer to others as a friend.

- Let your thoughts pass through your consciousness like clouds passing through the sky. Be in the present moment when the sky clears.

- When you find your thoughts preoccupied with speculation about the future, don't berate yourself. Gently remind yourself that you exist only in the here and now.

- Think your human thoughts, no matter how silly, paranoid, or irritable. Notice your assumptions and smile. Then let them go.

- Practice the gentle letting go of distracting thoughts. Do not judge yourself or try to figure out why you were thinking or what you were thinking.

- Voluntary simplicity is not just what you do, but also the intention with which you do it.

- Becoming aware and watching your anger or jealousy is a way of taking the seat of consciousness. Start by watching. Be aware that you are aware of what is going on inside. That awareness of the thought will prevent a harmful reaction.

- There is no need to worry that a good idea or the solution to a problem will be lost. What is of value will be available at the proper moment.

- Aim at letting go of thoughts. During meditation, open the hand of thought that is trying to grasp something and simply refrain from grasping. This is letting go of thoughts.

- Resolve to take two or three days to carefully notice the intentions that motivate your comments, responses, and opinions.

- Every time a problem arises, the important thing is to immediately become aware that the problem comes from your selfish mind, created by self-cherishing thoughts.

- Do not believe in something solely because someone has told you so or because of tradition or because many others believe it. Test for yourself, experience for yourself.

- Resolve to do a routine activity, such as making lunch, mindfully for a week, noting the thought and intention before each component of the action.

- For the purpose of meditation practice, there is nothing worth thinking about.

- Judgment is actually just a thought, a series of words in the mind. If you pay attention, you may be surprised to find that you judge practically everything. Count your judgments, like counting sheep.

- Mental manipulation of outer experience is your way of buffering reality and experiencing the world "according to you." You recreate the world within your mind because you can't control the world.

- You get locked into your view, which you take for reality. You think others should have the same view, but that's impossible.

- Say no to negativity. Negativity can be self-fulfilling. So if a negative thought crosses your mind, immediately change it into a positive one.

- Strive to avoid doing harm indirectly with your thoughts, judgments, attitudes, and intentions. These thoughts affect you internally and influence how you interact with others.

- Trying to change yourself, thinking that you have to do something about how and who you are, comes mostly from a sense of unworthiness, a sense of personal distrust. Become aware of this thinking without judging it and you will start to let it go.

- Thoughts about pains, rather than the pains themselves, cause suffering.

- Give yourself time for a long bath. Do not hurry. Let every movement be thoughtful. Be aware of each part of your body and of the water. Follow your breath.

- An insult becomes yours only if you choose to accept and engage it. It is the same with all your thoughts and feelings.

- A minute of thought is worth more than an hour of talk.

- We know our stories inside and out and backward and forward; thinking about them does not teach us anything. Quit rehearsing in your mind and indulging your stories.

- Whenever you feel stuck, frustrated, or limited, become aware of where your thoughts are dwelling. Then focus on something else. Do this over and over. Then focus on the breath and dwell on nothing at all.

- Take a moment's break and drop all doing— all thinking, all concentrating, and all contemplating. Just be at your center.

- What one feels, one perceives. What one perceives, one thinks about. What one thinks about, one mentally proliferates. Thoughts then become actions. Become attuned to this whole process.

- To keep your perspective fresh and free of bias, make a deliberate effort to encounter a wide range of ideas on issues.

- Detach from your thoughts by saying to yourself: *The mind is now thinking.* Each time you notice a new thought pattern, you are seeing the thought, not identifying and getting caught up with it.

- Renunciation does not mean you cannot drive a nice car, wear well-made clothes, or go out to dinner a couple of nights a week. Renunciation is renouncing mindlessness in carrying out these activities.

- We tend to internally verbalize the world, judge, complain, and decide what to do about it. In the world of thought, we mistakenly feel that we can do something to control our experience.

- Focus on traveling well instead of thinking that it is important that you arrive. Live life like playing a game. There are goals to give it direction, but the true aim is to enjoy playing.

- Becoming aware of every body sensation, sound, and mood as it unfolds in the moment helps you control attention and better face troubling thoughts.

- In meditation, you can learn to let the process of thinking stop by itself. If a thought crosses your mind, let it come in and let it go out.

- Break the habit of thinking that the solution to your problems is to fix or reorder things outside. The only solution to your problems is to go inside and let go.

- Before you get up, take some time to reflect on what it means to wake up and meet the day.

- When your mind tries to dwell on negative things, take time to sit quietly and silently clear your head. Think of a clear, flowing brook with fresh water gently cleansing and refreshing you.

- Pay close attention to your motivations and intentions—asking yourself *Why?* before you watch TV, drink alcohol, or do anything.

- Become aware of yourself by letting things go: emotional states, opinions, and passing thoughts.

- What you are today comes from your thoughts of the past, and your present thoughts build your current and future life. Your life is the creation of your mind. Right Thought integrates reason and emotion as well as understanding and will.

- Compassion allows you to transform resentment into forgiveness and fear into respect.

- Practice the art of ageless thinking at every opportunity, with regard to both yourself and others. Let go of conventional notions of how people of a certain age are supposed to act.

- Benevolence is silent good will, streaming out indiscriminately into the world—into your life.

- Spring-clean your brain, get to know yourself again, and learn how to pay attention. Attention, attention, attention.

- Think through what your day would have been like if you had not thought that some of it should have been different.

- Your monkey mind jumps around to make you feel better or worse about what has gone on in the past, what is occurring now, and what might happen in the future. Try to settle it down and become present.

- Persistent and insistent craving can be managed just like any other harmful habit of thinking.

- Right Thought means thinking kindly and refusing to engage in cruel, mean, covetous, or otherwise nasty thoughts. If nasty thoughts come up, let them go.

- Whatever arises in the way of thought or emotion can be accepted and worked with—without fear or reactivity.

- Don't give voice to any and every passing feeling or thought.

- There is no pushing thoughts and feelings away. They are there and can do what they like, but you should not engage them.

- One benefit of sitting meditation is that as you sit more and for longer sessions, your thinking becomes slower.

- Avoid saying automated greetings, responses, or compliments. Think of your own ways to express how you feel, tailoring them carefully to fit the situation.

- Stop from time to time during the day and pay attention to your inner dialogue. You are not your thoughts and you need to get used to *not* believing the messages they give.

- The stop sign is a reminder to slow your pace, take a moment's rest, and look around.

- When you realize that you are thinking about a pain, notice the thought, return to the physical sensations of the pain, notice the thought, return to the physical sensations of the pain. Does the pain ease for you?

- When giving advice to others, have compassion and thoughts for their benefit.

- What if you did not bring your inner
  mental voice with you everywhere you go?
  Real spiritual growth occurs when you stop
  doing this. Once you no longer identify
  with the mental voice, you are free.

- Our minds barrel along with a running
  commentary on everything, a constant
  judging of everything and everyone.
  These stories create separation and a
  sense of self and, therefore, suffering.

- Right Thought acknowledges unskillful
  feelings and thoughts such as anger and fear
  as they arise, then lets go of them.

- There is a big difference between drinking
  a cup of tea while being there completely
  and drinking a cup of tea while thinking
  about five other things.

- Be very watchful of your thoughts, for
  they are subtle and potentially dangerous.
  Luckily, the very act of watching changes
  them.

- Try this focus sentence in meditation:
  I think, but I am not my thoughts.

- Each like and dislike creates a web of
  thoughts. Meditation helps you cut back
  the desires and aversions so you are less
  often entrapped in the web.

- After meditation, hold the intention of
  moving through your life with awareness
  of each moment.

- Identify your inherently pure state of
  the mind unsullied by thought. See the
  luminous, knowing nature of the mind.
  With mindfulness, practice remaining
  in that state.

- When performing a chore, such as clearing
  the snow, try focusing all of your attention
  on your hands. Note the sensations. If a
  thought comes, let it go and refocus on
  your hands.

- One of the greatest challenges is resisting thoughts that are self-judgmental or tainted with negativity.

- Intuition shows you that your brain is not just a thinking machine. Keep your intuition sharp through the constant practice of awareness.

- Recall again and again the benefits of developing an intention to become enlightened for the sake of others.

- Intrinsically, all living beings are complete and whole, endowed with virtue and wisdom, but because of delusive thoughts they fail to perceive this.

- Once you have reacted, you are lost and imbalanced. You are carried away by the reaction because it has put you under the power of the thought. This is the normal cycle of thinking and the reason why habits are so difficult to break.

- When asked a question, pause sixty seconds before answering. Since the pause is obligatory, the likelihood is that the answer will include reflection, examination of intention, and a wise response.

- When envy or jealousy arises, mindfully cut through these "stories" in your mind. Letting go of the suffering that these stories generate, you will see things as they are.

- Become the witness. When thoughts have been dropped, joy will come.

- Work to endure anger or sadness by letting such feelings pass without ruminating on them or trying to change them.

- Instead of being carried away by your thinking, worries, or anxieties about the future or regrets about the past, dwell fully in the present moment, fully aware of each step you take.

- Renounce or detach from unskillful thought, ill will, and harming, from greed, hatred, and delusion.

- Be awake and aware without letting the mind move in relation to what it sees.

- During your meditation practice, rather than trying to tune out annoying clamor in your head, simply observe it. See the thoughts come and go. Don't judge them or let them engage you.

- By mindfully taking responsibility for and modifying hurtful intentions before they become actions, you will recognize and remember that you have the potential for positive transformation.

- The purpose of your life is not just to solve your own problems and find happiness for yourself, but to free every living being from all their suffering and bring them to full enlightenment.

- Go outside and scan the sky for one star that appeals to you or attracts you. Focus on the star. Think about what it is. Close your eyes and hold the meaning of your star inside of you.

- We are constantly shoveling more things into our minds—things to remember, to react to, or to think or worry or obsess about. Throw away the shovel; be happy and experience life as it is.

- When we eat, we usually think. You can enjoy eating a lot more if you practice not thinking while you eat. Just be aware of the food.

- Undertake for one week to act on every single thought of generosity that arises spontaneously in your heart.

- Look through the thought, not at it.

- The wise person makes steady his wavering thoughts before he acts.

- Do your best to return to your breathing one more time than your mind wanders. It does not matter how many times you get caught up in a thought or for how long. Begin again and bring awareness back to the breath.

- By letting go of all you believe you are, by letting go of thinking you are the body or the mind, that you are brilliant or stupid, and so on, you become whole and awaken.

- Two simple words, yes and no, require the most thought before use.

- If happiness comes, don't become too excited. If sorrow comes, don't become too depressed. Happiness and sorrow are not you. Watch, unattached. Happiness and sorrow depend on your own mind, on your interpretation.

- Make every attempt to leave your mind in its present, natural state, without thinking about what happened in the past or what could happen in the future. Let thoughts flow through, until your mind becomes like clear, still water.

- Even your smallest, least significant thought ripples throughout the universe. Be aware of the snowball effect of your thinking.

- A mind full of preconceived ideas, subjective intentions, or habits is not open to things as they are. Practice clears your mind.

- The most reliable and effective way to relieve problems such as anger, anxiety, and depression is to alter harmful habits of thought.

- Tame your mind so that you may bring peace and well-being into your heart and the hearts of all beings.

- Every morning, your first thought should be a wish to devote the day to the good of all living beings.

- Happiness cannot come from without. It must come from within. It is not what you see and touch or what others do for you that makes you happy; it is what you think and feel and do, first for others and then for yourself.

- Every time you reject a weak or negative thought because it's unworthy of you, you create space for something better.

- Think of your lunch break as a mini-vacation—an opportunity to connect with your nonworking self.

- If you're totally focused, you'll be aware of nothing but the object of awareness. Only when you pause will you realize how hard you've been concentrating.

- When you are concentrating on a specific task using your powers of observation, you are not thinking or worrying about anything else. You are practicing living in the moment.

- To stop the song in your head that stubbornly refuses to leave, go back to the breath and let go of the song. Intentionally practice letting go of this song.

- There are countless opportunities to make choices and modify your fate in creative ways—even to change the way you think. Visualize yourself as a creative artist, working with the raw materials of mind.

- Drink a cup of tea. Do not think about drinking a cup of tea. Just drink it. Feel it. Enjoy it. That is experience beyond thought.

- Look at everything as though it is the first time you are looking at it. Look at life like a child. See the magic in life.

- You can be lost in your thoughts and fears or you can remember to breathe, to soften the heart, to trust.

- Disregard whatever you think yourself to be and act as if you were absolutely perfect— whatever your idea of perfection may be. Behave as best you know how and do what you think you should.

- With your thoughts, remain an observer. With distractions, remain an observer.

- Instead of engaging or picking up on a thought or feeling, let it just flow by. Instead of letting every thought or feeling be the cause of action, let these impulses be energy to become aware.

- Every moment and circumstance in life is an opportunity for you to experience things as they are, not as you fear or wish them to be.

- Challenge yourself to think about a dreaded chore as a possibility for happiness.

- Just because you have the painful feeling of being a failure does not mean you are one. Emotions are impermanent and deceptive. View failures as victories in wisdom.

- By learning to hold your mind to an object in meditation, you train in patience. Then, when a moment of anger arises in your everyday life, you may be able to hold your speech and action.

- Criticizing yourself, judging somebody else, thinking you need to change, to fix something, or to improve, is a problem.

- There is a big difference between taking a walk in the woods and really being there, and taking a walk while planning dinner or imagining the stories you will have about your walk.

- Rather than identifying with your thoughts, take a step back and observe them.

- With mindfulness and awareness, you can pry your mind away from fantasies, chatter, and subtle whispers of thoughts.

- Right Thought tells you that when you face fear, you need to do whatever is necessary to bring yourself into the moment. You can do that by bringing awareness to your breath or another mindfulness object.

- Restrain yourself from acting on angry impulses. Patience means buying time with mindfulness so that you can act rightly.

- True seeing is what you do simply by glancing at the world around you, taking in the details of what you are looking at. Why verbalize or narrate with the mental voice what you have already seen? Unskillful thought is a habit.

- Remember all the bad advice your mental voice has given you that has caused you suffering.

- Take a day, or a few days, to just be silent. Turn off the TV, the radio, the telephone, even the thoughts in your head. Do not read, write, or surf the Internet. Take refuge in the calm and peace of a quiet mind. Keep still.

- The Zen approach to thought is to acknowledge it rather than deny it. Thoughts given control can block your creativity and ability to communicate. Engage thoughts with lightness and playfulness, with an attitude that they don't have power over you.

- Learn the art of stopping—stopping your thinking, your habit energies, your forgetfulness, the strong emotions that rule you.

- Anything worthwhile requires restraint and a certain amount of sacrifice. Making sacrifices to attain the greatest happiness is always better than going after trivial pleasure.

- If you begin to understand that thoughts are thoughts and feelings are feelings, you will become less invested in the drama that your thoughts and feelings can so easily create. You will begin to live more gracefully.

- Thought manifests as word; word manifests as deed; deed develops into habit; habit hardens into character. So watch your thoughts and their ways with care. Let them spring from love, born out of concern for all beings.

- Live by Buddhism's precept of Right Thought. Refuse to assume anything about anyone and use your power and authority gently.

- While sitting and breathing, think of yourself as a pebble falling through clear water. While sinking, there is no intention to guide your movement. Sink toward a resting spot on the gentle sand of the water's bottom.

- One way to work with large thoughts is simply to bring yourself back to the room you are sitting in.

- If you are able to let go of your thoughts during meditation, you will find that the mind can settle down with a much greater sense of satisfaction in its state of concentration.

- Instead of acting and reacting impulsively—following your thoughts and feelings here, there, everywhere—watch your mind carefully, and try to deal skillfully with problems as they arise.

- You may feel guilty about eating too much or not enough, or worry about eating the "wrong" things. These feelings are just as damaging as the foods. Whatever you eat, eat it with full awareness and joy for every bite.

- Feeling sorry for yourself or wishing things were different in your life only increases the amount of suffering you experience. Stop wanting things to be different than they are.

- Reflect on what is truly of value, what gives meaning to life. Set your priorities based on that.

- Do not spend time lost in thought, judgment, fantasy, daydreams. Pay attention to direct experiences of sight and sound, smell and taste, and bodily sensations.

- If one thinks that one is happy, that is enough to be happy.

- Be aware of the times in meditation when you think: *Am I doing this right? Is this what is supposed to happen?* Hold those questions in awareness without trying to answer them.

- Just do what you are doing without thinking about it. Just be where you are without holding on or running away. Give up judging and spectating and dive into this moment.

- You can make plans and even hope for certain things to happen, but you must avoid clinging to even the thought of a specific outcome.

- Have an ease and openness of mind that receives with interest every kind of circumstance. Ask what you can learn from each experience.

- You do not need to indulge the mind's every desire and impulse. Learn to say no to the mind, gently and with humor.

- Help others purely for the sake of helping, with no thought of personal gain and without wishing to be recognized for it.

- When you are full of desire or fear, or are nervous, the mental voice goes into high gear. This is easy to see when you feel anger. The mental voice goes off on the person over and over before you ever even see the person.

- When you live in the present moment, you can be aware of your intentions and can see their causal relationship with your words and actions.

- By being attentive to the feelings, intentions, and thoughts beneath your words, you learn to cultivate the compassion, integrity, and kindness that bring harmony to your relationships and to your mind.

- Set an intention for your day, such as *Today I will be a good listener* or *Today I will not get distracted*. Repeat your intention to yourself whenever you tire or lack motivation.

- Do not wish to be anything but what you are, where you are, right now. Learn to wish that everything should come to pass exactly as it does.

- Compassion is not the same as pity. Pity is the feeling you have for the homeless man begging. Compassion is understanding that all of us are in this situation together.

- You can alleviate your own suffering by alleviating the suffering of others. Stop thinking about your own problems: go and do good for someone else.

- Staying calm and stable while paying attention is the key to resolving differences and misunderstandings.

- Recognize worry for the traitor it is to your peace of mind, and rely instead on positive but realistic thinking.

- Much of the time our minds tend to drift freely from thought to thought. This can compromise our enjoyment of passive pursuits, especially those involving listening or being a spectator.

- If you are not caught up in thoughts about your experience, then it is simply experience. It is living in the present moment, in truth.

- Your words should be in harmony with your thoughts and intentions.

- When you are tempted to buy another pretty sweater when your closet is already full of them, ignore the thought and divert the mind. Replace the greedy thought with a generous one; reflect mindfully on the impermanent nature of sweaters.

- Appreciate the diversity of beings you encounter. Like flowers, they bring beauty, variety, and sustenance to your world.

- Just being aware of the mind that thinks it knows everything is a major step toward learning to see through your opinions and perceive things as they actually are.

- If you are fully present in the moment, time will be suspended. The feeling of being trapped or overwhelmed will evaporate.

- Pay as exquisite attention as possible to your every thought and activity from moment to moment. This will help you to stop, and it ultimately becomes a different and profound way of life.

- Watch your thoughts—they become your words.

- The more you are mindful of your thoughts, the more concentration and insight you will have, especially into the nature of your own suffering and the suffering of others.

- Everything has implications—every thought, word, and deed has an effect; absolutely everything you think, say, or do makes a difference.

- When you cannot stop thinking about something, first think about the best-case scenario. Then think of the worst-case scenario. Then let it go and wait for whatever comes.

- Live by the precept of Right Thought by refusing to assume anything about anyone or anything. Assumptions are thoughts you believe.

- If you have an awareness of your feelings as feelings, it becomes possible to break out of the passive or hostile modes that you automatically fall into when feeling threatened.

- A way to deal with recurring obsessive thoughts is to call them repeats. Every time one pops into your head, say to yourself: *Repeat*. Noting desires with humor can help get your mind out of its rut.

- Watch out for continuous trains of thought or lists going on in your mind. Let the mind rest on the breath and on life itself.

- Change happens one breath at a time, one thought at a time.

- When you explore feelings of superiority and find a way to end them, you allow empathy, loving-kindness, wisdom, generosity, compassion, and awakening to enter your mind and heart.

- Experience the wavelike motion of thinking. Riding the wave of thinking, focus on the space between thoughts.

- When your thoughts leave your mind in the form of speech, if Right Mindfulness continues to accompany them, you know what you are saying and whether it is useful or creating problems.

- Do not permit your mind to wander aimlessly. Always be mindful of your thoughts, the way you are mindful of your actions and speech.

- If you're constantly thinking about what you'd rather be doing—getting off work, driving a different car, or eating dessert, your mind is starving for mindfulness.

- Write the words "What Am I Doing?" on a piece of paper and hang it where you will see it often. It will help you release your thinking about the past or the future and return to the present moment.

- *Ahimsa* is the yogic practice of nonviolence. It also means not having negative or violent thoughts, and being gentle and patient at all times.

- See confusion for what it is and don't get stressed by it. It will pass. To apply rational thought to confused situations can sometimes feel like using the wrong tool for the job.

- Disclose the countless misdeeds of mind you have perpetrated with an intent to harm others. Regret having done this and intend to abstain from this in the future.

- Take loving-kindness breaks throughout the day—sending out good and taking in bad. See what a difference you can make simply by intending to help others.

- Renounce your tightly held opinions and open yourself to what is.

- Hold your seat. Stay centered—not moving, not reacting. Allow your thoughts and impulses to come and go. Release your illusions.

- If you have "no-mind," all your thinking and feeling won't get between you and the work you have to do. If you have no-mind, you lose your ego. You become your doing. You let go of your preconceptions about yourself, your life, your work—and find that your mind expands.

- Be as aware as possible of your thoughts and emotions so you can prevent harsh speech.

- You are what you think. Pain will follow bad thoughts as certainly as happiness will follow good ones.

- Forgetfulness is the opposite of mindfulness. You walk, but you are not paying attention to walking. You are someplace else, thinking about the past or the future.

- If you're reading an instant message and talking on your cell phone while thinking about things you need to get at the store, you're not doing any of these things fully. The antidote is mindfulness.

- Watching thought is letting go of the content as you become aware of the process, seeing the space around each object of the mind.

- You are nourished or depleted just as much by your thoughts as by the quantities of protein, sugar, calories, and so on that you consume.

- It is extremely important to Right Thought that you realize you are not the mental voice, you are the one who hears it. Much of what the mental voice says is meaningless, a waste of time and energy.

- You may believe that it is difficult to let go, but in truth it is much more difficult and painful to hold and protect. Anything you grasp ahold of is surrounded by fear and defensiveness.

- When you enter a meeting, keep an open mind and be patient. Do not allow your thoughts to wander; be exactly where you are, wait your turn, and contribute.

- When there is an inward awareness of every activity of your mind and your body, when you are aware of your thoughts, of your feelings, both secret and open, conscious and unconscious, then out of this awareness comes clarity.

- Thinking may give you a sense of control. If you think over every possible outcome, you believe you can avoid a negative outcome. If you think about all the ways to handle a situation, you believe you will handle it better. If you think, think, think, you will have control, right? It is better to understand your motivations and act from that point. Overthinking or ruminating does not offer you control over outcomes.

- It is normal to feel moments of doubt in which the attention wanes and resolve weakens. Acknowledge doubt and be alert to sabotaging thoughts. This will help you let them go.

- Treat discursive thinking and obsessive thoughts like old audio tapes that you are now bored with. When they start, ignore them and return to the present moment.

- You are not your thoughts. You can observe them and be aware of them without becoming identified and caught up in them.

- If you dwell on bad thoughts, then your life will be full of negativity. If you don't allow bad thoughts, you will be free of all things negative.

- Acknowledge that the contents of your thoughts are not facts.

- Write the words "Are you sure?" on a piece of paper and hang it where you will see it often. Wrong perceptions cause incorrect thinking and unnecessary suffering.

- If you're thinking about a pain in your body, notice the thought, and then return to the physical pain itself. Don't make it worse by letting it invade your mind.

- When the mind is soft and nongrasping, you don't get caught in the melodramas that cause pain to yourself and others.

- Do not judge yourself harshly. It is like judging the sky for its weather. Self-acceptance and spacious awareness allows you to experience your precious life as it is.

- Ask yourself: *Does this thought create suffering or well-being?* You will find that you have created much of the suffering yourself in your own mind.

- Instead of thinking about doing something, do something.

- Watch when the waves of negative feelings and thoughts wash over you. Accept their presence. Observe the turbulence. Move into the eye of the storm. Watch the storm die down and be replaced by a calm mind.

- Being aware of, being the witness to, an inner disturbance is better than losing yourself in an external reaction. There is always a next problem and your aim is to respond, not react.

- Mindfully examine your opinions and rigid conceptions with an open heart and clear mind. Your attachment to your opinions is a key source of suffering. Let go.

- If you cannot find tranquility, peace, and love within yourself, it will be difficult to find it elsewhere. Whittle away your self-hatred with loving-kindness.

- Remedies for negative thought: Ignore it.
  Divert the mind to something else. Replace
  the hindrance with its opposite. Remember
  that everything changes and is
  impermanent.

- Try labeling thoughts as useful or not
  useful. Or try categorizing them: *This is a
  worry. This is a memory. This is something
  I should do.* Notice if doing this helps you
  gain understanding of your habitual
  thoughts.

- You get more joy out of giving joy to others
  and should put a good deal of thought into
  the happiness that you are able to give.

- Make the effort to let go of compulsive,
  obsessive thoughts. Notice repetitive
  thoughts and familiar stories you tell
  yourself. Label them and return to the
  object of your concentration.

- Become aware of your breathing and of what feelings or thoughts are passing through you. Just by doing that, you may quickly calm down and the urge to speak mindlessly may pass.

- When you notice negative thoughts arising, observe them without judgment before replacing them with more positive thoughts.

- Be careful not to take your own inner landscape for granted.

- Cultivating balance in your life can help you get in touch with your inner self. Every day—think a little, feel a little, move a little, rest a little, eat a little, drink a little, sleep a little, and meditate a little.

- Distress or unhappiness can trap you in a vicious circle: you feel bad about yourself, which gives you a negative view of your predicament, which makes you feel worse.

- You can only have the highest happiness by having thoughts and feelings for the rest of the world as well as yourself.

- When you wake up each morning, reaffirm your intention to practice loving-kindness and compassion. Remind yourself each day to let go of ego clinging, selfishness, controlling behaviors, negative thoughts, possessiveness, aggression, resentment, and confusion.

- Study the cause-and-effect relationship between intention in the mind and movement in the body.

- For a healthy outlook, examine what is going on in your mind, checking your motivation and intentions.

- A major obstacle to enlightenment is feeling cheated, holding a grudge about who you are, where you are, what you are. Let go of these feelings to overcome this obstacle.

- Thoughts in your mind are expressed through the mental voice. Your mental voice was created as an inner environment that you believe is under your control. That is an illusion. Don't believe that mental voice!

- Meditation is difficult because the mind is in the habit of attaching to thoughts, feelings, ideas, opinions, expectations. Meditation substitutes a more benign caretaker, watcher, or observer for the obsessively thinking mind.

- The sense of well-being that comes with repeatedly bringing your mind to a state of calm and stillness begins to permeate everything else in your life.

- When you learn to label thoughts in meditation, you will be able to label thoughts as wholesome, profitable, skillful, or otherwise in daily living also.

- Attachment to an expectation that creates a sense of self sets up the condition of suffering. This can be something ranging from a child rejecting a dish you prepared to a partner you love rejecting you and leaving.

- It is important to have pure intentions and express yourself from the heart. Be patient and prepared to persevere.

- Note your thoughts and feelings when they arise, but especially note any move to avoid or push away what you do not like. Welcome these thoughts and accept them; get a feel for accepting and letting go.

- A minute of extra thinking beforehand can save hours of worry later.

- Notice that your thoughts about the past and future are only thoughts. You are thinking about them in the present. Notice that. Is there a point to these thoughts?

- When your mind is burning up with thinking, don't feed the fire with fresh thoughts. Let it burn out naturally in meditation.

- Choose to express only those thoughts that will bring happiness to yourself and others.

- Pursue every activity with this single intention: Be gentle, kind, thoughtful, caring, compassionate, loving, fair, reasonable, and generous to everyone, including yourself.

- Your mind is constantly seeking satisfaction, making plans to ensure that things will go your way, trying to get what you want or think you need and ward off the things you fear, the things you don't want to happen.

- Moments of stillness and genuine simplicity offer glimpses of what it means to live in a spiritual and free way. You know you do not need yet more sounds, thoughts, experiences, possessions, or attainments. You actually have a thirst for freedom and stillness. The clutter of your life and mind entangles you in alienation, exhaustion, and haste.

- All the happiness in the world comes from thinking of others; all the suffering in the world comes from thinking only of oneself.

- You want a mind at rest, with no thoughts of desire or aversion, so that in each moment you see things as they are.

- On your path to enlightenment your thoughts will often turn to the divine. Approach the concept with as few preconceptions as you can.

- You may think that if you give up the illusion of control, you'll miss out, lose, fall behind. But giving up something you never had can only clarify your life.

- Use the gift of vision to recognize without discrimination the ingredients of your world. Be mindful about imposing good and bad attributes upon what you see.

- When you are mindful of the process of thought itself, you can more readily catch your own lapses of mind, the inaccuracies in your thinking, and the behaviors that follow.

- Direct your thoughts and energy toward realizing your dreams for the future. Visualize your success.

- The next time you feel irritable or inexplicably angry—stop, sit down, and think about what is really bothering you. Try to address the real problem.

- During the day, stop at times and pay attention to your inner dialogue. Watch the thoughts like a tennis player watches the ball. You do not have to believe the messages they impart.

- Think of an activity that you associate with being calm, such as lying in the sun or taking a warm bath. When you feel under pressure, think about such a relaxing activity.

- Putting down the burden of craving will improve your happiness. Freeing yourself from your unquenchable thirst for things and pleasures will give you more energy, creating a refreshing calm in you.

- Stopping thoughts is about as effective as trying to have a relationship without fighting.

- The next time you feel yourself going into a downward spiral, turn inward. Instead of distracting yourself with something, sit down and breathe. Meditate and let things be.

- If painful thoughts or memories arise, simply observe them and let them go. The same goes for pleasant thoughts. Remember that all thoughts are impermanent.

- Cultivate flexible thinking. Cultivate thoughts that hasten the development of wholesome qualities.

- The happiest people are those who think the most interesting thoughts. Those who decide to use leisure as a means of mental development—who love good music, good books, good pictures, good company, good conversation—are the happiest people in the world.

- Notice the intentions that motivate your speech. Direct your attention to the state of mind that precedes talking, the motivation for your comments, responses, and observations.

- Your mental health is not defined by the content of your thoughts, but rather by your relationship to the content of your thoughts. Observe your feelings and thoughts and have compassion for yourself.

- It is easier to behave your way into a new way of thinking than to think your way into a new way of behaving.

- To wake up means to free the mind of its habitual disease of uncontrolled thoughts.

- The next time you find yourself at a lake, pond, river, or ocean, listen to the white sound of the water. Enter into the flow of the water and let it wash everything away. Let all your thoughts fall into the water and dissolve.

- Bring a self-judging thought into your mind. Let the thought become the object of your attention. Soften around the pain of the self-judging thought. Label self-judging thoughts whenever they come up during the day.

- Create positive thoughts that support the immune system. Quietly surrender to the process of healing and send your body the gift of loving thoughts.

- You are working toward breaking the internal dialogue, the constant comment of the mind, breaking through where the thinking occurs and directly experiencing the process.

- When you touch base in any moment with the part of your mind that is calm and stable, your perspective changes immediately. You can see things more clearly and act from inner balance.

- Instead of trying to stop your judgments, practice the simplest form of awareness: notice your thoughts and beliefs as they arise and inquire into their truth.

- Think of yourself as a cat or dog, completely relaxed in front of a warm fire. Feel that your muscles yield without resistance to anyone's touch.

- Stay aware of the flow, of the fact that everything is in ceaseless change. If you remain open to experience and change, you will find yourself able to deal with life's different weathers.

- The Buddha pointed us toward three skillful thoughts: generosity, loving-kindness and friendliness, and compassion.

- Any time you experience disappointment, this has come from delusional thinking. You are not accepting things as they are. You are attached to an outcome.

- Think of the chores you face in the day ahead as a privilege, not a burden. Resolve to enjoy the satisfaction of doing them to the best of your ability. Take pleasure in your skills.

- That we take ourselves so seriously, that we are so absurdly important in our own minds, is a problem for us. It is pointless to take ourselves too seriously. Life is too short.

- Happy people think happy thoughts.

- All the objects that we perceive in life are created by ourselves. Our perceptions of objects are based on the time and place we are in and will be different from everyone else's.

- Perform a meditation when listening to someone else. Still your mind and open your heart to fully hear the other person. Concentrate: do not be distracted by your own thoughts and emotions. Hear the other person with acceptance and compassion.

- Notice how your mind tries to flit away to yet another thought or image. This helps you break deeply habitual patterns.

- The important aspect of Right Thought is insight, the ability to see things as they really are. The opposite is delusion.

- You have to unlearn being concerned with thoughts.

- Thinking is less interesting than looking.

- Let each in-breath calm your mind and body, and let each out-breath release any tension or thoughts you are holding.

- Find something in your life that you are afraid of doing, such as a fear of making a phone call. Do it today, not thinking about how. Just do it. Do this every time you face a similar limiting situation over a week and look at how that feels.

- Ask: What am I doing? This will help you overcome the habit of wanting to complete things quickly and automatically. Smile to yourself and say: *Washing this dish is the most important job in my life.* If your thoughts are carrying you away, you need mindfulness to intervene.

- Nothing can help you or hurt you as much as the thoughts you carry in your head.

- Remember that you are not in charge of life and you cannot control what people think of you. You are not in charge of anything, and when you realize this you will be free to really live.

- Do not fixate on stress or trauma—just let go. If you don't attach to the things that cause you stress, they can't cause you stress.

- A habit of mind is like eating junk food. Once you start, it's hard to stop. Preventing negative thoughts from arising is hard. Once you are hooked, it is difficult to let go.

- Forget what others think of you. Forget the goal of achievement. Arrive instead in your mind-body, attending to the present moment.

- Know you are breathing in. Know you are breathing out. Be aware of thoughts arising and passing away. Be aware of your judgments about thinking. Realize the suffering your judgments cause you and smile with compassion. Dwell in the present moment.

- Choose a response instead of being carried away with a reaction.

- *Mantra* means literally "tool for thinking." The repetition of sacred words and phrases has been used since the earliest times to purify and focus the mind.

- Mindfully attend to your breath. You will find that mindfulness of the breath can tell you much about your emotional state. The breath can bring you into the present moment and be used to calm your mind.

- Your prospects will brighten with an influx of positive thoughts.

- Very few decisions are right or wrong—except in your own mind. You may mistakenly suppose that something like the choice of a college can make you happy. The real truth is that happiness comes internally, not from something external.

- If you are able to maintain continuous mindfulness, nothing will upset you. You will not become angry or agitated. You can be patient no matter what anyone says or does. You can stay peaceful and happy.

- Anything that can be written in a book or that can be said—is thinking. But if you read with a mind that does not add its own thinking, then you read the truth.

- It is beautiful and peaceful to stay in a place of silence of mind. Discover the blessing of inner silence.

- You do not have to look outside yourself to find great happiness. You can find it inside. Your treasure house is in yourself. It contains all you will ever need.

- Sometimes the best way to feel your feelings or think your thoughts is to sit in silence. When you do, you are less distracted and can be more fully aware of the essence of your feelings and thoughts.

- The answer to very real problems can often be worked out, even thought through, more skillfully when the mind is allowed to quiet. Be willing to listen for the answer.

- Feeling trust and seeing the basic goodness in others and yourself has healing power.

- Resentment only poisons your own heart while doing absolutely nothing to the intended target. Let resentment go.

- Imagine an alien from another planet with the power to look inside a human mind. The emotions, sensations, thoughts, and feelings would be fascinating. Think about that.

- All the kinds of fear share the characteristic of not being in the present moment but in the future.

- It's sometimes tempting to believe that if you think about a problem for long enough, you will resolve it—but all that happens is that your anxieties deepen. Don't fall into the trap of endlessly rehearsing the same old issues. Let things go for a while.

- Every time you think of helping someone else become more generous and giving, you plant very powerful seeds within your own mind.

- Letting go is a way of letting things be, of accepting things as they are. Let go, on purpose, of thoughts of the past or future.

- Read a book you know you'll disagree with: there's no better way to sharpen your thinking.

- When you interact with the world, the mind naturally interprets the events, and your thoughts become your reality. You fall into a trap where your mind creates the world you perceive. You can address this through meditation and mindfulness practice.

- Each thought, each feeling creates the world. Hold joy and suffering tenderly in each breath.

- Hold a pebble in your hand and focus your attention on it. Look at the grain and the variations in hue. Feel its cool hardness. Close your eyes and squeeze it and think of a dream or a goal. During the day, hold the pebble in your hand and focus on the dream or goal.

- If you really want to understand your mind, you must watch it while it is angry, while it desires, while it is in conflict. You must pay attention to the mind as the thousands of thoughts and emotions arise and fall. When you pay attention to your emotions, you will find that they lose their strength and eventually die out.

- Nothing is half as important as you usually think it is.

- Once you have encountered how you are feeling and thinking, then you can express yourself honestly and clearly.

- Imagine your mind as a clear blue sky, and each thought as a passing cloud. Let each cloud drift by without your judging or otherwise positively engaging with it. Just observe.

- When an opportunity comes, do not let it pass by, yet always think twice before acting.

- A mind beyond judgments watches and understands. A moment of recognition about judgmental mind is a moment of freedom and wisdom.

- When thoughts come or melodies go through your head, be glad for them. Then bring your attention back to what you were doing.

- Thought is a dialogue with yourself, adding a personal spin to experience. Be aware that what your thoughts add to a situation is not the truth of the matter, but a fiction influenced by your experiences and personality.

- After you have spent some time watching thoughts and emotions come and go, you begin to see them clearly. They no longer have the power to destabilize you, because you see how ephemeral they are.

- Seeing crises and threats as challenges and opportunities allows you to heal.

- On a shoreline, collect some rocks, pebbles, or shells. Think of habits, fears, resentments, and beliefs you are ready to let go of. When you are ready, toss a rock, pebble, or shell into the water and let it carry with it the thing you are ready to let go of.

- While it's important for some plans to be well thought out, leave room for courageous spontaneity.

- Discover that thoughts are not the enemy.

- Be aware of a thought as it arises in your mind. Be aware of the end of a thought as it passes out of your mind. Be aware of the space between the thoughts in your mind.

- Be mindful of everything you think, and learn to change your thoughts from unwholesome to wholesome.

- Do not reject thought, sound, sensation, or anything that arises in meditation. Accept it, acknowledge it, and let it go.

- Mindfulness is being purposefully aware and noticing what you are experiencing and your response to those experiences. By living fully in each moment, you focus your effort on the present instead of insisting on what the future must be.

- Reflective or analytical meditation is choosing a question, theme, or topic of reflection and focusing on it. When your attention wanders, you return to the topic or question.

- Stop what you're doing for a minute and think about the sensations in your body, your relationships with others, your mind and spirit. You've momentarily relieved yourself of the burden of habitual thinking and have taken a step toward awareness.

- Start the day by reaffirming your intention to practice loving-kindness and compassion. Remind yourself to work at letting go of ego-clinging, selfishness, possessiveness, aggression, resentment, confusion.

- Overcome fear by shifting your concern from yourself to others. When you see the difficulties that other people face, your own fears seem less important.

- Watch what your inner voice has to say when you are exercising or going on a walk. It talks nonstop. It jumps from one subject to the next, never letting up. This shocking realization frees you from it.

- Be free from judgment of others and of yourself. Let such judgments come and go without getting caught in them; experience the dance of life without critical thoughts of how it should look.

- Try to leave your mind vividly in a natural state, without thinking of what happened in the past or of what you are planning for the future, without generating any conceptions. Let the mind flow of its own accord without conceptual overlay. In time, the mind will appear like clear water.

- Your thought patterns and beliefs are stories that you have been telling for a lifetime. Who is this storyteller? Without the stories, what or who are you?

- Taking time each day to meditate helps you to find a center from which you are able to deal with the changes and waves of daily life. You become more oriented and stay on your path.

- In meditation, by putting distance between yourself and your thoughts, your mind becomes relaxed, flexible, workable, pliable—and you have more clarity about your direction in life.

- Starting in the morning, notice what the mental voice is saying in every situation—for every person you interact with, every time something changes or a sound occurs. Just try to watch each comment it makes.

- Think of the power of nature—the way new life is conjured from seeds and other small beginnings. Then turn your mind to the power of your own thoughts, which are equally powerful.

- Cultivate the stability of a mountain, strengthened by the insight this viewpoint brings.

- Shake off all worries and anxieties, not thinking of the future, not thinking of the past, just enjoying the present moment.

- It doesn't matter what anyone else thinks or does, because you can't control what anyone else thinks or does.

- Remember: with your thoughts you make your world.

- We tend to perceive what we have learned to see, based on conditioning and memory. Unless you make a deliberate and conscious effort to see things as they are, you miss many beautiful objects and scenes in life.

- Progressively release habitual patterns of thinking and behaving.

- You scratch without realizing that you itch—seldom noticing the intention that activates the body's movements.

- Gradually drop your ideas of who you think you should be, who you think you want to be, or who you think other people think you should be. These thoughts distract you from living a joyful life.

- Those who don't give a thought to what others think tend to be the most revered.

- Your thoughts are just thoughts—they are not you. They are a type of baggage you've picked up along the way. Drop the baggage and run with joy!

- When you try to stop your thinking, it means you are bothered by it. Thoughts in the mind are like waves to the boat captain; if you are not bothered by the waves, gradually they become calmer. If you see the thoughts but are not pulled by them, your mind becomes calmer.

- Your suffering is generated from within your own mind. Fixed opinions make you feel self-defensive and anxious; cravings make you feel frustrated and dissatisfied.

- Think of a cat, asleep much of the time yet acutely aware of what is going on around it. The cat is simply being itself wholeheartedly. It is in the present moment, open to whatever occurs.

- Ego hides a person's delusive thinking, greed, and anger.

- In between meals, try to notice the moment just before you reach for a snack. That is the subtle moment when your mind has formed the intention to eat. Noticing that moment will enable you to be much more aware. If you still want the snack, enjoy it mindfully.

- The Zen approach to worry is simple: just don't do it. No matter how much you worry or fret over something, it never helps the situation.

- Instead of trying to think through and plan everything out, dive into the present moment and tap into a wellspring of nonstop intuitive guidance.

- Thoughts intermix and influence your experience of the world. Instead of real, unedited experience, you get a narrated version, a personal presentation of the world according to you.

- We feel justified in being annoyed with everything. We feel justified in thinking we are more clever than other people. Self-importance hurts us, limiting us to the narrow world of our likes and dislikes.

- When you have control of your mind, driving the speed limit is a natural thing to do. You do not feel anger, frustration, or rage at what is happening around you on the road. If you have control at the wheel, most likely you will have control in other areas of your life as well.

- In sitting meditation: notice the thought, return to the breath, notice the thought, return to the breath.

- Thoughts have a way of amplifying external difficulties, ideas of inadequacy and loneliness, and feelings of rejection, leading you deeper into delusion. By choosing to transform your mind, you can weaken this delusion and not be enslaved by your thoughts.

- View information through insight. Try to develop both intellect and intuition. Read widely, think deeply, and retain your sense of discrimination.

- Unrealistic expectations tarnish your appreciation of life, weighing down the buoyancy of the present moment.

- All suffering is caused by ignorance. People inflict pain on others in the selfish pursuit of their own happiness or satisfaction.

- When you put others at the center of your life, it releases your natural desire for happiness and liberates you from your self-centeredness while helping you to enlighten your heart.

- If you recognize worry for what it is, acknowledge it, put it in perspective, and refuse to let it control you—that's cultivating spiritual living.

- Don't worry about what other people are thinking of you.

- If worry is a major part of your thoughts and fills your mind whenever you're not actively concentrating, it may be habitual. Discard all those niggling concerns and feel pure, light, and focused.

- See that there is no use for the constant internal chatter and no reason to continually attempt to figure everything out. The real problems in life are caused by the mental voice, by unskillful thought—trying to change the past, present, or future by sheer thought.

- Take in each sight and object as it presents itself. Try not to label or think about what you see. Be aware only of a sense of shape, color, and presence of everything in space and time. Acknowledge that everything you see is actually taking place, moment by moment, inside your own mind.

- Be cautious in what you believe and think of others.

- Become more aware of the room and the noises—and the silences between the noises.

- A simple mindful exercise that you can do when you are waiting in a long line is to take a break from your usual thoughts and complaints and wake up and look at the magical and vast world around you.

- When you change who you are thinking you are and what you are thinking you deserve—you find that the world around you changes simultaneously and that experience is more real.

- Do not chase after thoughts, and don't push them away. Just let them come in and go out like a swinging door. Stay in the moment and see that a thought is just a mind formation.

- Remain mindful and awake rather than being carried away by thoughts and projections.

- Each person has an awareness, an inner witness of the source of that person's own intentions. Each person also has a mental voice—the part of that person that is never quiet. Getting rid of the latter brings peace and serenity.

- Neutralize a negative thought by substituting a positive one for it. Raise yourself up to a higher spiritual perspective by remembering that everything happens for the best.

- Kind hearts are gardens, kind thoughts are roots, kind words are flowers, kind deeds are fruits.

- Generosity is the willingness to give, to share, to let go. Love is the inspiration, and in giving, you feel more love.

- There is a big difference between the pain of pain and the pain you create by your thoughts.

- Think of the slow driver in front of you as protecting you from driving too fast.

- Contemplate the positive qualities of an experience, even a bad one, and refrain from saying or doing anything that might cause further damage or escalate anger.

- Beautiful thoughts are free.

- All living beings are Buddhas, endowed with wisdom and virtue, but because people's minds have become inverted through delusive thinking, they fail to perceive this.

- Your conversation is the mirror of your thoughts.

- The mind is like a puppy, wandering endlessly and delighting in each new distraction. An antidote to distraction is concentration.

- You burden yourself thinking that happiness consists of certain things. When you leave aside your limited views, it is possible to open up to deeper experiences of joy.

- Magical things happen every day, if you allow them. Think of daylight, of the stars at night, a flower, a weed; the list goes on and on.

- Fantasizing or daydreaming in moderation
  is fine. But don't spend too much time lost
  in fantasy. Stay in touch with reality.

- Pay attention; it pays off. Stay conscious of
  what you say and think. Mindfulness keeps
  negative tendencies in check.

- A thought is like a cloud, appearing, being
  seen, and then moving on to another part
  of the sky.

- When you acknowledge your intentions and
  take responsibility for them, you have the
  genuine possibility of transforming yourself.

- Remind yourself that it is your thinking
  that is negative, not your life. This
  awareness is a step toward happiness.

- You don't have to do anything about
  unskillful thoughts, but you have to become
  aware of them and the predicament they
  put you in.

- If you catch yourself being paranoid or taking things personally, question the logic of it. Is somebody really trying to annoy or hurt you? Or are they simply going about their business or being oblivious or ignorant toward you? Irritations and annoyances can be unpleasant, but you do not need to take them personally or react to them.

- Contemplate, remember, and study spiritual teachings that can help your mind go beyond temporary situations in which negative thoughts arise.

- When you are swamped by anxiety, it can be tempting to dwell on thoughts of escape to somewhere else, where you can be happy. An external change of scene can help you find perspective, but it won't solve deep-seated problems. It is better to find an inner oasis through meditation and relaxation.

- Whatever you do, direct your intention to benefiting others.

- No matter what you have done, said, thought, accomplished—you have this capacity inside of you for transformation and it can bring lasting happiness.

- If you feel confused and disconnected, meditation will help. The heart and the mind gently release. You feel less overwhelmed and become more effective, more relaxed.

- Standing back and noticing your thoughts helps you see the habitual patterns in your thoughts and reactions. You now have a chance to change them.

- Your mind is a room where you rearrange thoughts out of habit and ignorance. You move the thoughts in a desperate attempt to get things just right, so that you may satisfy yourself.

- By acknowledging your intentions and taking responsibility for them, you have the genuine possibility of transforming yourself.

- An unwholesome or negative state of mind cannot arise at the same moment as a moment of mindfulness.

- In your thoughts, you meet the burdens of judgment and blame, the endless replaying of the past and rehearsals of the future. Thoughts are not living in the present moment.

- Ask yourself: *Who am I?* Make the mind as empty as space, totally unattached to phenomena. When thoughts appear, become the question: *Who thinks these thoughts?* Keep asking the question, but abandon the answer.

- As soon as a thought arises to distract you, acknowledge it and kiss it good-bye.

- Thinking is creating a reality instead of directly experiencing what is happening each moment.

- You cannot think something that has already happened into not having happened.

- A good way to pray is to ask that the person you are praying for receive what he or she needs most at this time. You can pray in this way for yourself, too.

- Pay attention to the thoughts, images, and memories that cause sadness for you. You can then open to your own suffering and hold the sadness with compassion and loving-kindness.

- Many of the people who cause us the most stress may be people we love dearly. We need to take responsibility for our part in those relationships, for our own perceptions, thoughts, feelings, and behavior.

- Thoughts are little stories you tell yourself. Most of them concern the past and future, not the present.

- Sitting back and noticing your thoughts helps you see habitual patterns. Use the insight of meditation to change them.

- Notice thoughts having to do with fear. Fear arises from anticipating the future and imagining not being able to cope with it. When you see fear for what it is and come back to the present moment, fear starts to disappear.

- Think of all the people and hard work that contributed to creating an object, from raw material to finished product. Take a few minutes to appreciate these people and the work they did.

- Think of your attachments as being like boxes of unneeded items stored in an attic. In meditation, go to the attic and remove each box and put it in the garbage. Feel a sense of lightness as you let go of these attachments.

- Any time dark or negative thoughts enter your mind, point a bright light to chase them away. Make your mind a sanctuary for sunny, positive thoughts.

- Think of yourself as complete, like a seed or a bulb. All that you seek lies within. To live a life of peace, you need nothing more.

- You may find difference unsettling and feel anxious in a world of different viewpoints, different temperaments. Rejoice in difference, rather than seeing it as a threat.

- Gaze deeply at something until thoughts disappear.

- Breath will cut through thinking because you have to let go to breathe.

- Charging headlong through life, without stopping for silent thought, is one way to ensure that the object of your quest will elude you.

- The more you are concerned about the happiness of others, the more you are building your own happiness at the same time.

- Self-absorption rules thoughts and intentions. It is thinking about everything in terms of your own interests and concerns.

- Your mental voice is talking because you are not okay inside. But even when you are not particularly bothered by anything, it still talks, narrating your world. The mental voice is a habit to make you feel more comfortable, an illusion that you are more in control of your world.

- Tolerance enables you to refrain from acting angrily to the harm inflicted on you by others. Tolerance protects you from being conquered by hatred.

- Recognizing what you do with your mind and how delicious whatever you're doing can be—these insights make even the most mundane activities delightful and nourishing.

- You can renounce driving a fuel-inefficient car. You can renounce buying clothes you really do not need. You can renounce ordering both an appetizer and a dessert as well as an oversized entree. These are harmful activities.

- Sit in meditation, inside yourself for a while, in complete solitude and silence. You will almost instantly hear incessant mental chatter. You generally don't notice it, but meditation makes it clear. This is one of the most important insights of meditation.

- The best way to bring peace to the world is to bring peace to ourselves through meditation and mindfulness practice.

- One enlightened thought and one is a Buddha; one foolish thought and one is again an ordinary person.

- Do not try to keep thoughts from coming up or try to push them away, but also do not cling to them when they do come up. Thinking is normal, but believing the thoughts is unnecessary. Let each thought arise and pass away without struggling with it.

- You may be thinking it's time for another cup of coffee and one of those blueberry muffins. You think there is always something to do other than be in the moment.

- Decide not to narrate your world and, instead, consciously observe it.

- Practice acting on thoughts of generosity that arise in your mind.

- Press your tongue against the upper palate—apply all your energy to overcome a bad thought.

- View meditation as a process without a clearly defined outcome. This way, you create a space in which to sit with yourself, quietly observing your feelings and thoughts, allowing yourself to be.

- Pay attention right now to what you are sensing and feeling. Whenever your mind flits away to another thought or image, relax and come back to the present moment.

- Find a situation that is troubling you and which you have been trying to work out. Think about it and *do nothing.* Stop all unnecessary activity and thoughts. Take a walk and enjoy the moment. After a period of time doing this, note the changes that have taken place without your doing anything about it.

- Observe whether your mind is quiet or whether thoughts begin to flow. Are these creative thoughts or judgmental ones? Are you accepting the world as it is or are you dissatisfied?

- Your mind is like a swinging door. Thoughts and feelings come in and go out like someone through a swinging door. Be the door, not the doorman. The doorman becomes engaged with the thoughts and feelings. The door simply observes what goes in and out.

- If you listen carefully, you can learn from the most subtle whispers of thought and sensation as well as from the most overwhelming feelings and emotions.

- Gently let go of distracting thoughts. Do not judge or try to figure out why you were thinking this way or that, or whether these thoughts will return.

- Mindfully take responsibility for and modify hurtful intentions before they become actions.

- Thinking about thinking is not meditation.

- Right Intention is the intention to be free from desire, to not harm or be cruel.

- Watch every thought that passes through your mind. Watch every desire that takes possession of you. Watch every act that you do. Let everything become an opportunity to watch. When you watch, clarity arises. The more watchful you become, the more your chattering mind becomes quiet.

- Your object in meditation is not to stop the mind but to develop a healthy relationship to the act of thinking.

- Make it a point to be happy, to be here and now. The first thought of the day should be positive and special.

- Seeing the scope of your wanting frees you from grasping, from thinking that all your wants have to be satisfied, that you have to compulsively respond to everything that arises in your mind.

- Be careful not to dwell on painful memories or to indulge in pleasant ones. Remember that all thoughts and experiences are impermanent.

- The power of silence is that it teaches you to listen. Listening wholeheartedly includes receiving the feeling, emotion, and intention beneath the words.

- Most of us are addicted to thinking. Just say no to thought. Watch the waves of thought instead of getting caught up in the content of thought.

- Control the menu of thoughts and images that flash through your mind. Dwell on the positive things and they will inspire you.

- Think long-term. Remember that satisfying short-term desires will never make you deeply happy or satisfied with life.

- Awareness is your true self; it is what you are. You need to notice how you block awareness—with thoughts, judgments, expectations, and so on.

- All that we are is the result of what we have thought. If a person speaks or acts with an evil thought, pain follows him. If a person speaks or acts with a pure thought, happiness follows him, like a shadow that never leaves him.

- Work toward less desire, avoiding unnecessary activity, not wandering in the world of desire and not thinking irrelevant thoughts.

- Regard each day as a good day. Stop to think why you say good morning—and use this meditation to always say good morning and mean it.

- Focus on what you are doing, being mindful. This frees you from thoughts of winning or losing and allows you to execute tasks effectively.

- Each time your attention wanders, notice the thought that distracted you, then gently return to the activity. Notice the thought, return to the activity; notice the thought, return to the activity.

- Think of yourself as a charioteer, and your emotions as horses under your control. They are powerful and can be headstrong, but if you train them properly they'll usually submit to your will.

- Do not be afraid of mistakes; you can always correct them. Only intentions matter.

- Stop the constant internal dialogue. You are free because you are not thinking about the past or future. You are enjoying the activity.

- Pay attention to your thoughts—but do not mistake them for who you are.

- Recognize that positive thinking is a powerful force in achieving your goals.

- Take time to be alone on a regular basis, to listen to your heart, check your intentions, reevaluate your activities, thoughts, and words.

- The only way to find peace and contentment is to stop thinking about yourself.

- When your mind is completely open, you have plenty of inner space for creative thoughts to bubble up from their source.

- Beginner's mind is a mind that is willing to see everything as if for the first time.

- Emotion is a creation of your mind. It is thought turned into a seemingly solid entity.

- Meditation will help you identify the luminous and knowing nature of the mind, unclouded by thoughts and without any concepts overlaid on pure experience.

- Change your thoughts and you'll change your mood.

- Being grounded means being completely attentive no matter what you are doing.

- Don't let your thoughts be controlled by greed, ill will, or delusion. This only intensifies your own and other people's suffering.

- Forget about big compassionate thoughts. Just be kind on this breath. Be kind to the one who breathes.

- Each time you acknowledge a fantasy or thought, you are softening your mind by becoming less bound to concepts and emotions.

- Contemplate every decision based on how it will benefit others.

- To ward off bad dreams, try meditating on an image that you associate with happiness and peace for a few minutes before you go to bed.

- See that nothing in life is permanent. Your thoughts, feelings, and perceptions all pass. If any particular thought catches you, gently release it and simply continue watching.

- When negative thoughts weigh you down, imagine each of these thoughts as a bubble. The bubbles slowly float out of your head. Let tension float away with each bubble.

- Whenever you experience great disappointment, you are attached to expectations of a specific outcome. If you don't build your world on expectations, it does not collapse when things turn out differently.

- It is not easy to stop thinking, but focusing on a sound or image can help. Repeat a mantra or gaze at a candle flame or mandala.

- Pick an object and look at it without thinking. Then slowly withdraw your eyes and remember its essence.

- Try giving inspiring thoughts that occur during meditation a label as they arise, such as "brilliant" or "Einstein." This method acknowledges a thought you would like to retain, but then allows you to let go and go back into the meditation.

- Mentally prepare for sleep. Focus on calm thoughts. Banish nagging worries by meditating.

- Take a step toward inner peace by accepting whatever is happening in the present moment. Silently say yes to your feelings and thoughts, to the sensations within your body, the sights you see, and the sounds you hear. Allow what is there to simply be there, without wishing for it to change in any way.

- Happiness is the confidence that pain and disappointment can be tolerated, that love will prove stronger than aggression.

- Call a time-out whenever you feel distress. Take slow, deep breaths. Replace thoughts that reinforce distress and arousal with a thought about something that makes you feel happy.

- Concentration aims at unwavering focus on the chosen thing or idea to the exclusion of any other subject. It is complete one-pointedness of thought upon the subject at hand.

- In walking meditation, keep your mind totally focused on your environment, not on the thoughts that try to distract you.

- Once you have begun to see that the self is distinct from its thoughts, its sensations, and its experiences, you start to be less anxious about mortality.

- Have no thoughts of good or bad and be free from suffering, desire, and impurity.

- Discipline moves us beyond the ignorance of thinking that we can do more or less what we want.

- Feeling strong emotions is a part of life, and there is nothing wrong with them when you learn to relate to them skillfully instead of becoming obsessed with them.

- Empty your mind of premade thoughts. Only when you dump out your teacup can you make room for the really good tea.

- Emotions are a part of our lives. When you calmly investigate the emotions that spring up in you, you see that they are impermanent. They come and go.

- With practice, it can become second nature to think of the positive things in life rather than the negative things.

- Appreciate each moment as a vehicle for developing wisdom.

- Learn to recognize the signs of worry—distraction, obsession, repetitive thoughts, insomnia, compulsive eating, nervous behavior. Step back, sit down, and watch what is going on inside your head. Worry is a habit distracting you from your true self.

- Simply notice your feelings and thoughts. Question their truth.

- Learn to live fully in the moment, rather than being lost in dreams, plans, memories, and commentaries of the thinking mind.

- Let go of the thought: *I am this body.* Let go of the thought: *I live in this particular time and place.* Let go of the thought: *I am I.* Let go of your thinking, your attempts to control the world.

- Embrace your difficulties and appreciate them for providing new ways to grow spiritually. Try to think of the positive benefits and spiritual lessons that troubles can almost certainly provide.

- You never do anything well till you cease to think about the manner of doing it.

- Keep your private thoughts private.

- Deal with ill will toward someone who consistently treats you poorly and inappropriately by generating loving thoughts. Wish happiness and love to all beings, even to the specific person you may be angry with.

- Before going to bed, meditate on your place in the universe. You are safe and you are loved. Think about what you want the night to teach you.

- A great deal of your suffering comes from having too many thoughts.

- Thinking is the speech of your mind. Right Thinking makes your speech clear and beneficial.

- If you cannot accept yourself and treat yourself with kindness, you cannot do this for another person. Make friends with yourself. Then you will be making friends with others.

- If you start to think that what you are doing is silly or that you don't want to do this, simply observe the thought and let it go. You do not have to indulge these thoughts.

- Picture a person or animal clearly in your mind. Think about the things you most love and appreciate about this being. Let your heart be filled with the love and affection you feel.

- In an emotionally charged situation, focus your attention on the physical sensations in your body and on your own emotions, not on the situation or on other people involved. If you feel tension, bring your attention to that. Breathe and relax. Open yourself to find a creative solution or response to the challenge.

- In walking meditation: notice the thought, return to the walking, notice the thought, return to the walking. Let go of all thoughts and allow whatever emerges to be.

- You are very often driven by your likes and dislikes, totally unaware of the tyranny of your own thoughts and the self-destructive behaviors they often result in.

- Even if for a single moment you are not doing anything and you are just at your center, utterly relaxed, that is meditation.

- Notice the silence between sounds and the space between thoughts.

- Antidotes to suffering, stress, and anxiety include resisting less, grasping less, and identifying with things less.

- Discard all the words with which you think and stay in quietude.

- The sticky, repetitive places your thoughts return to are messengers asking for your attention.

- A thought precedes every action. A right thought precedes a right action.

- In observing thoughts, it is important not to comment or judge their content, but to see them as they arise. This way, you do not fool yourself into believing the voice in your head.

- Practice being interested in doing this very simple thing in the moment. Think of each moment as a one-pointed concentration, focusing on one aspect, this one moment.

- Stop comparing yourself and setting yourself up for unhappiness.

- Mindfulness gives you the time you need to prevent and overcome negative patterns of thought and behavior and cultivate and maintain positive patterns. It gets you to turn off the automatic pilot and helps you take charge of your thoughts, words, and deeds.

- Generally, if you worry about your situation, you complicate it, adding mental anguish to physical suffering.

- The habit of always thinking about yourself only makes you unhappy. If you want to be miserable, think about yourself. If you want to be happy, think of others.

- Concentrate and nurture your mind with your best thoughts.

- In meditation, be aware of the short space between the end of one thought and the start of another. Look for this momentary pause, no matter how brief. Try to rest in this space.

- Learning to watch your mental voice talk through meditation is the beginning of a wonderful inner journey, a spiritual awakening.

- Use your willpower to catch every negative thought that passes through your mind. See them, don't judge them, then let them go.

- Find a way to punctuate your life with thought-free moments so you create little gaps that take your mind off automatic pilot. Whether through deep breathing, meditation, pausing, or listening, wake up and see the amazing world around you.

- Meditation allows you to look at the problems that thinking creates for you, the little traps your mind sets, where you get caught and stuck.

- If you master the mind, you will have mastery over body and speech. This is done through constant awareness of all your thoughts.

- Patience has three essential aspects: gentle forbearance, calm endurance of hardship, and acceptance of the truth.

- Have the courage to let a thought slip by and not chase after it. By not clinging to a thought or rejecting it, the mind will open to a natural awareness.

- No matter what your mental voice says, it is still just a voice talking and you listening. You may like or dislike what it says, but it is not you.

- You hide behind the stories you tell yourself and others to get what you think you want. This just makes you feel incomplete and alienated from your authentic self.

- When you start thinking you are having a good time, the good time is usually over.

- Exploding myths about who you believe yourself to be requires a radical rethink. Ask yourself what myths you live by and start removing the delusions.

- Your words are your thoughts with wings. You open your mouth and your mind flies out.

- One simple way to detach from thoughts is to say to yourself, *The mind is now thinking*, each time you notice a new thought pattern. This will help you to stop identifying so strongly with your thoughts and help you feel what witness consciousness is like.

- When you are aware of your intentions in the present, you can shape your future.

- Feelings are not facts. We create a lot of suffering for ourselves and others when we act on feelings that we believe are facts.

- Sitting in silence is full of potential wisdom. Feeling uncomfortable or threatened by silence is no excuse for filling all your time with thoughts and words.

- Generally, people don't experience what is going on but, rather, think about what's going on. Meditation is the way to cultivate direct experience and let go of thinking.

- On cold winter mornings, don't start thinking about getting up or what the day holds. Keep your mind quiet, and channel all your energy into jumping wholeheartedly into your day without thinking about it.

- When you are not attached to who you think you are, life moves through you and you experience the present moment. Understanding continual change, you release your attempts to control circumstances.

- We tend to continually drift around in our own thoughts, not properly attending to what the world is offering.

- It may not seem like it at the time, but the root of your suffering is found internally. It comes from the limitations you have placed on yourself, not from some outside force. It can have no negative effect on you unless you allow it.

- In meditation, when you lose awareness of your breath, you have retreated into analytical thinking or discursive thought. Your conscious breath will bring you back to your mind-heart-body.

- Diplomacy is thinking twice before saying nothing.

- Whatever you are doing, wherever you are, keep attentive to the gap between the in-breath and the out-breath. You will recognize two layers of existence—doing and being.

- Unless one is mindful and knows what one is saying, one should keep quiet and try to find out what one is thinking.

- The certain way to be wrong about a journey is to think you control it.

- Try the exercise of counting thoughts, observing and making it a part of your mindfulness. The power of awareness should be strong enough that you will not get caught up in the content or story of each thought. The thought comes, you observe and count it, and it passes away.

- You have feelings, but you are not those feelings. You have thoughts, but you are not those thoughts.

- Even something as simple as wrapping a gift can be a meditation. Do everything with thought and precision, and meditate on the joy of giving.

- Your mind makes everything. If you think something is difficult, it is difficult. When you do something, just do it.

- Improve your karmic lot by reframing how you respond when difficult outer events come up. See challenging situations as your karma. Do not fight too hard against challenging times.

- Embrace all animals with your compassion. Wish for your compassion to ease their suffering. Protect life, practice generosity, behave responsibly, and consume mindfully.

- When you see how often your mental voice changes its mind, how conflicted it is on so many topics, how overreactive it is, would you listen to that voice if it was someone on the outside? How many times has your mental voice been totally wrong?

- People always try to accumulate more and more, thinking that these things are essential for their existence. In fact, stuff may be obstacles that prevent us from being happy. Release these things and become a free person.

- When strong emotions arise in your life, find refuge and stabilize yourself through your breath. By going to your breath, you can feel the calmness that breathing deeply provides.

- Once you control your thoughts, which wander all over the place if given the chance, you will escape the clutches of temptation.

- Keep a journal of the types of thoughts that predominate in your mind. This will help you let go of unskillful thoughts and cultivate skillful ones in your life.

- If your mind is obsessed by compulsive thinking and grasping, simplify your meditation practice to just two words: LET GO.

- Meditate on the value of throwing out mental garbage that you no longer need or want. Be willing to leave behind beliefs and patterns of thought that no longer work for you. Imagine your mental garbage discarded.

- In the morning say to yourself: *I will avoid causing harm through my thoughts. I will do my best to nourish well-wishing thoughts for all beings.*

- Being lost in thought is the problem, not thinking itself.

- Shed your desires and hatred. Be at peace in thought, word, and deed and let go of all attachment.

- When thoughts or images of the suffering of another being arise, bring your attention to your heart, letting yourself be touched by the pain and feeling loving-kindness and concern.

- As enlightenment grows in you, confusion and ignorance will have to withdraw. This will influence not only your thinking, but also your body and your way of living.

- When you truly love yourself, you begin to know yourself better and realize what good you are capable of doing.

- If you are feeling anxiety, first notice how anxiety is spinning its wheels. Then say to yourself: *I am sick of thinking about this. Instead of feeling anxious, here are three things I can do.*

- We think so much, yet we truly know and understand so very little.

- When you are grounded in calmness and moment-to-moment awareness, you are more likely to be creative and to see new options, new solutions. You become more aware of emotions and less carried away by them, and you can maintain your balance and perspective in trying circumstances.

- Make your thoughts the object of mindfulness. Immerse yourself in your thoughts and follow their interconnections. Detach yourself from your thoughts and simply observe their movements. You'll begin to see that you are not your thoughts, and therefore you need not be ruled by them. They change and you can choose to ignore them.

- When thoughts of pain and hurt begin to overwhelm you, sit and make yourself smile. Just sit and physically and mentally make yourself smile.

- The step of Right Thought is variously translated as Right Intention, Right Resolve, Right Aspiration, and Right Motive. The reason for this is that there are various kinds of thoughts that constantly bombard us.

- See negative thoughts, but don't judge them. And then let them go. Neutralize each negative thought with a positive one.

- Ask yourself: *What am I waiting for to make me happy?* If you develop the capacity to be happy in any surroundings, you will be able to share your happiness with others.

- Delight in the positive coincidences in life, such as an old friend calling just as you were thinking of her. We are more connected to each other than we might think.

- When you become attached, you are deluded into thinking that something can belong to you or that you can control it. Everything is changing and there is nothing you can truly possess or have full control over.

- If you hate someone, it is because you hate those same feelings or tendencies in yourself. If you judge someone, it is because you judge yourself in the same way.

- If you spend your time hoping that it will not rain on the weekend, you are wasting your time. Your thoughts do not change the weather. Your thoughts do not change anything.

- Freedom from thought does not mean no thoughts. It means that thoughts come and go freely and you don't latch onto them.

- Once you learn to notice exactly what is happening, you can observe your feelings and thoughts without being caught up and carried away by your typical patterns of reacting.

- See if you would like to let go of unskillful thoughts and cultivate skillful ones in a particular area. Use this insight for a week to remind yourself of these positive intentions.

- Whenever you find yourself ensnared in negative behavior, you should increase the amount of time, thought, and energy you direct toward positive behavior.

- There is almost nothing that your inner voice says that you do not pay full attention to. It pulls you out of reality, even if it is enjoyable, and you pay attention to whatever it is saying. You don't tell it to stop; you listen. If someone outside of you said these things, you would ignore them. Why do you feel you owe your inner voice this attention?

- Anger arises from the same self-centered conditions as fear. Anger is not good or bad, but expression of anger is almost always unskillful.

- Before a meal, you can join your palms in mindfulness and think about the people who do not have enough to eat.

- When you are at your most agitated, the pressure of inner unrest seems to unlock your mouth, as if saying your every thought is the only way to reclaim inner calm. This is not helpful and fuels further agitation.

- Take in the bad, send out the good. Breathe out, thinking all your good fortune goes to others.

- We are fools if we think that harsh language ever accomplishes anything positive.

- True renunciation involves rejecting any thought, intention, word, or action that causes suffering to yourself and others.

- Everything is created by your consciousness, by your perception of life. The trick is to maintain this awareness as you live and act.

- Take a few moments each day to think carefully about the good things you have.

- Observation of thought means reflection on the workings of your mind. Observation of thought is fundamental to spiritual practice.

- Think about the irony of being angry about feeling angry, or guilty about feeling guilty. Recognizing and accepting old conditioned emotional reactions helps change them.

- Being mindful means being constantly aware of your feelings, your surroundings, what your own body is doing, and what thoughts and ideas you are experiencing.

- An amazing tool is being able to just let things go, to not be caught in the grip of angry thoughts, passionate thoughts, worried thoughts, or depressed thoughts.

- Right Understanding, Right Effort, and Right Mindfulness run and circle around Right Thought. The Noble Eightfold Path is really a wheel or a circle with no hierarchy or order.

- The true mind comes into being when the mind does not dwell on any thought.

- Be willing to be objective and watch all your thoughts. You will see that the majority of them have no relevance, no effect on anything or anybody.

- One of the blessings of cultivating loving-kindness is that your thoughts are pleasant.

- The desire to become something other than what you are creates suffering.

- By thinking of yourself less, you learn to love yourself more.

- Letting go of who you think you are allows your life to soften.

- By cultivating positive thoughts, you create the cause for a happy, peaceful state of mind.

- Sit with an intention for a while before deciding whether or not to follow through with it. Sense the feelings involved with the motivation. The more fully aware you are of the intention, the more you truly have a choice in acting on it.

- Analyze your life closely. If you do, you will eventually find it difficult to misuse your life by seeking money or stuff as the path to happiness.

- Let go of your desire for the end of suffering. Instead, focus on this thought: *Whatever difficulties life brings, I will not be anxious about them.*

- Mindful awareness, rather than merely thinking, can lead you to wisdom and to a happiness based on what is true.

- The next time you drink coffee, instead of spacing out or doing it automatically, turn it into a meditation. Pay close attention as you sip. Whenever your mind drifts off, bring it back to the experience of your coffee.

- Take a favorite passage from spiritual literature and read a few sentences or paragraphs, just enough to read about the spiritual truth but not enough to start analysis in your mind. Note how the passage affects you. Don't think about it or analyze it in the usual way. Let it marinate in you.

- Letting go of thoughts at the end of the out-breath is like moving a large rock away so that water can keep flowing.

- Reflective time provides a chance to focus inward and listen to the wise voice within. Clarity ensues and problems may be solved effortlessly and effectively.

- Habits of thought can be critically examined. Most of the time your thoughts are pushed or pulled by delusion. See the aversions or desires in habitual thoughts and let the unskillful thoughts go.

- There is within us, much of the time, a critical judging voice commenting on what we're doing and how we're doing it, pointing out that we're not up to par, not being worthy of love. Ignore this critical voice; let it go.

- When you become aware of your thoughts, you will be surprised. Did a thought just run through your head? The very act of watching it changes it.

- Without anxious thought-construction and thought-projection, the mind would not jump from one thought to another. Without anxious thought, doing comes from being.

- Only you are responsible for the feelings and thoughts that arise. When you blame, you give up your capacity to choose and give up your freedom.

- Ignorant of the truth of dissatisfaction, we believe that a new job, new house, or new partner will bring us genuine happiness.

- Make kindness your religion, and it will spread to others. Kindness breeds kindness.

- Many upsetting thoughts and beliefs are simply bad habits. If you let your upset mind settle, your course to the road of happiness will become clear.

- Be aware of the short space between the end of one thought and the start of another. Look for this momentary pause, no matter how brief. Mentally attempt to rest in this space.

- White blood cells and trees don't think, they just do their work.

- Anger, like all emotions, is associated with sensations and thoughts that come and go. You do not need to be bound to it or driven by it.

- Experience the body as a mirror of the mind and discover how thoughts, emotions, and habits continually impact and shape the physical body.

- Suffering is caused by desire. Desire is wanting something you don't have, wishing something were some way it isn't, or being otherwise generally dissatisfied with the way things are in a belief that things would be better, you would be happier, life would be sweeter if only this were the case, if only that would happen, or if only something were different from the way it is now.

- If you have an imagination, you know that once you start imagining negative things, they start happening. If a negative idea comes, immediately change it to a positive thing. Say no to it, drop it, throw it away.

- A person is as great as his thoughts.

- Let a challenging situation go. Don't dwell on it or complain about it, especially when it will change and dissipate. You might create more bad karma with your thoughts.

• When the mind is continuously looking for something to entertain it, an unhealthy mental environment is created. This can distract you from development and impede your progress.

• It would be easier not to go to all the trouble of constantly ruminating over your suffering. It would be better just to sit in nature.

• Why should you believe and get involved in all the thinking that occurs in your everyday life?

• Let thoughts be light as bubbles, gently coming and going. They will pop on their own.

• Releasing the thoughts and returning to the breath gives you a sense of space and relief. You are grounded.

- We work to distinguish between the thoughts, *I am angry* and *This is anger*. You want to see that anger is present but not personal, breaking the cycle of attachment to the feeling that "you" are angry.

- Laughter can stop pretensions you detect in your attitudes or behavior and be useful in undermining stale, habitual thought patterns.

- When struggling with a difficult feeling, just sit with it. Try to identify the source of this emotion. Now gently let it go. If the thoughts remain, do not try to push them away. Let them fade like the light in the evening.

- Nirvana is the freedom from attachments to thoughts, feelings, and desires—and a complete and total absorption in the present moment.

- When you are with someone whom you find problematic, see if you can silently offer loving-kindness to that person while you are in his or her presence. Incorporate loving-kindness into your listening.

- If you spend some time observing your mental voice, the first thing you will notice is that it never shuts up. If you watch carefully, you will see it is just trying to find a place to rest. It is shocking to realize that your mind is constantly talking.

- When we observe life moment-to-moment (as opposed to spinning around inside our thoughts like a hamster on a wheel), we create a gap that allows us to notice what is happening instead of identifying with a thought about what is happening.

- Express your most positive thoughts and feelings. Tell others that you care about them.

- Meditation helps you learn to work skillfully and to allow thoughts, concepts, and perceptions to come and go as they please.

- Practice listening for the silences between sounds and noticing the space between thoughts. This allows you to enhance intuition and expand the range of your senses.

- Distancing yourself from the content of thought allows you to regain a sense of objectivity and freedom.

- Thoughts can make you more ill than any virus.

- Abandon thoughts of blame and hate, and live in love.

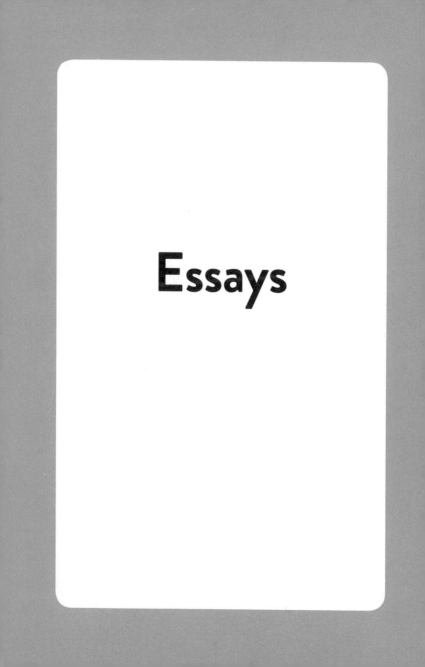

Essays

Actions and Consequences

Think about a problem you have, such as impatience or reactiveness, and then make a list of the thoughts that usually trigger the problem. Can you see how addressing the root cause—your thoughts—could solve the problem?

Right Thought is about taking responsibility for your thoughts and realizing how you believe them to the point that you let those beliefs control the way you respond to situations. By examining what goes on in your mind, you will discover that you are in control of what you believe about your experience. You do not need to believe thoughts that lead to harmful or nonbeneficial reactions.

Every thought, even ones that you consider small and insignificant, can have real consequences beyond your own life. By training yourself to focus on the thoughts behind your actions, you take responsibility for them. Start by setting a time during which you can pay close attention to your motivations and intentions regarding problems. Keep asking yourself *Why?* about any upsetting thoughts. If you think something that you do not feel good about, ask yourself why. If you train yourself to be mindfully aware of the whole context of your thoughts, you will cultivate the strength to be extra careful when you are vulnerable or very agitated.

Anger

Just before you express anger, note what has just transpired in your mind. This is especially helpful if you were going to write something like an e-mail or were going to leave a voice or text message. Pause for a few seconds or a minute and in your mind go over the thoughts leading up to this. Stopping or pausing the anger often lets you see that though you may get to blow off steam, you don't gain anything, even in that moment.

This is a preventive exercise. If you choose not to express anger, you do not have to expend the time and energy needed to repair any damage that your anger causes.

Think of the person or situation about which you feel anger. Hold that image and look at it from every angle. Focus on your role in this: Where were you wrong or thoughtless or mistaken? Imagine how you would feel if you were no longer angry or upset at the person or situation. Explore the possibility of making amends, offering forgiveness, or simply letting go of your resentment. Make a commitment not to harbor resentments in the future.

Anxiety

Happiness is not a brilliant climax to years of grim struggle and anxiety. It is a long succession of little decisions simply to be happy in the moment.

—J. Donald Walters

There are many times when each of us feels anxious about all that has to be done. Maybe it is the holidays, your workload, or family responsibilities. One way to address anxious feelings is to make a to-do list that you can work through. Your anxiety will decrease with every completed task.

Often, though, anxiety exists in a situation that you cannot control. There is absolutely nothing you can do externally about the issue or circumstance. Your anxious thoughts are not benefiting you here, so you will do better to look for ways to let go of the thoughts and return to a more peaceful state of mind. Make the little decisions to be happy in this moment and then the next. Enjoy the relief from anxiety that you can find in meditation. And take every chance you get to do something for others and get outside of your self-centered concerns.

Appreciation, Gratitude, Joy

The things you appreciate and are grateful for are good thoughts you can act on. If there are people in your thoughts, take time to let them know how you feel—such as by sending a letter or e-mail of appreciation or telling them you love them. Each day, you can share appreciation or gratitude with someone.

Keep a journal on your nightstand. Each night before nodding off, fill in the blanks with things you are grateful for. You will begin to look for things throughout your day to write down. This practice shifts your focus away from what is wrong in your life to what is right and beautiful and kind in the world. When you begin to think about things you are grateful for, you become grateful for more things.

Each day say, "I am awake and grateful to be alive." Be thankful that you can appreciate what the day brings. Once you get going, gratitude will overflow. It connects you to a state of appreciation that spills over into what you think, do, and say.

Aspiration

It is important to see that aspiration is not desire. Desire comes out of ignorance, whereas aspiration is based on Right Understanding, seeing clearly. It is not wanting to become anything, but rather is a feeling, an intention, attitude, or movement within us. Your spirit rises and you aspire to truth, beauty, and goodness.

Why are some people not completely happy even when they have a beautiful house, a car, the perfect marriage, lovely bright children? You may think, *Well, if I had all of that, then I'd be content.* But you probably wouldn't be. Until you realize that satisfying your desires does not bring contentment, you will not know the truth of real happiness.

Meditation is a way of deconditioning the mind that helps you to let go of all the hardline views and fixed ideas you have about your desires and your happiness. The contemplation of our human aspiration connects you to something higher. When you ponder and wonder about this universe you are living in, you see that it is very vast, mysterious, and incomprehensible. Your mind is receptive and open and you can let go of fixed and conditioned reactions you have about happiness and satisfying your desires. This brings you closer to true happiness.

Attitude

If you want to be a positive person, seek out people and activities with positive qualities. Surrounding yourself with their energy will help you achieve a more positive attitude and life. If you want happiness, take your future into your own hands. Actively seek positive influences that will help you achieve your fullest potential. Don't just sit in the giant barber chair, letting a stranger spin you and have free reign at reshaping your head. Choose your barber and your company carefully, and face that mirror. You are the one who has to live with it.

This includes surrounding yourself with positive friends and fostering relationships with people at work who have a positive attitude and effect; positive thinking is contagious. Researchers continue to explore the benefits of positive thinking and optimism on health. One theory is that this outlook enables you to cope better with stressful situations, which reduces the harmful health effects of stress on your body.

Periodically during the day, stop and evaluate what you are thinking. If you find that your thoughts are mainly negative, try to find a way to put a positive spin on them.

Start by following one simple rule: Don't say anything to yourself that you wouldn't say to anyone else.

Follow that with another simple rule: If you don't have something nice to say, don't say anything at all.

Meditation, along with other meditative pursuits like knitting, needlepoint and cross-stitching, watercolor and oil painting, cooking, writing, and creative hobbies and activities, are great tools for establishing a positive attitude and bringing you contentment.

Awareness

Self-awareness increases your self-confidence. You may not understand what is behind a hunch or an impulse, but mindfulness allows you to study motivation and intention. Instead of immediately acting on a hunch or ignoring an impulse, do a mindfulness practice. Listen to and analyze your impulses. Examine and consider following these clues and leads.

Give each moment your attention and awareness. The excitement of being alive will fill you. The world owes you nothing, but you owe the world gratitude for your life. Each moment should be a tribute to this gratitude.

Don't waste energy battling all the little waves—the ocean is full of them and they keep coming; just pay attention and correct the course when necessary.

As you wake up, welcome the new day with a mindful smile. Ask that you may live each moment with compassion and awareness. Ask that you walk on a path of peace and do no harm. Ask that you become more aware. Each day, spend some time in quiet contemplation of your own wealth of knowledge and talents.

Beneficial Actions and Thoughts

Spend time watching your thoughts, noting what they are—beneficial or harmful. Becoming more aware of the thought process is very helpful to your ultimate goal: happiness. Understanding the process helps you see that you are not your thoughts—that you can give thoughts a chance to settle down, and even let them go, and cultivate positive, loving thoughts.

You may think that what goes on in your brain is not part of your karma, but it absolutely is. There is a cause-and-effect with your thoughts as well as your speech and actions. Like your body, your mind needs training for optimal performance. By becoming more aware of your thought process, you are training yourself to have more control over your mind. When you have positive control of your mind, it can only have a positive effect on your happiness.

We think a lot about things we want to say, we meant to say, we need to say. It is good to have a filter, not to blurt everything out. It is good to consider timing and whether what you have to say will be beneficial or harmful. Mindfulness of your thoughts will take good care of your actions and speech. Mindfulness is informative and helps you cultivate the ability to let a thought slip by and not chase after it, so that you remain an observer, a witness.

Compassion

You have to generate love and compassion for yourself first. The nourishment that comes from being kind to yourself is the type of food that stays with you.

Develop a flexibility of emotional response. In the face of anger, for example, practice generating compassion toward yourself and others. In the face of greed, practice generating gratitude for all that you have. Experiencing jealousy, try finding a feeling of rejoicing in the good fortune of another. When impatient, practice patience.

As you gain more insight and grow spiritually, you begin to look at the world in a different light. You realize that you have a tremendous amount of control over how you feel and perceive the world. By generating a powerful feeling of warmth, loving-kindness, and compassion for all beings, you can train yourself in exchanging suffering for happiness. This can be done anywhere and anytime; you don't need any tools or devices, just the right frame of mind. By first admitting that you want well-being, you take the first step toward feeling genuine empathy for others. This allows you to adjust your thought process, which then lets you respond rather than react.

Cultivating Goodwill

Cultivating goodwill—friendly, helpful, or cooperative feelings—purifies the virtues of the person who develops it and brings the mind to Right Concentration. The power of goodness in a single person's heart can accomplish so much.

Goodwill is often a more skillful attitude than overt expressions of love. It is an attitude you can express for everyone. Even if the people around you haven't been acting lovably, it's good to remind yourself that although you don't condone their behavior, you still wish them well. Even for people you dislike, you can find it in your heart to wish them well.

Goodwill is a skillful feeling. You can promise yourself never to harm people again. Goodwill also acts as a check on your behavior toward those you love, so as to keep it from becoming smothering. It reminds you that people ultimately will become truly happy not as a result of your caring for them but as a result of their own skillful actions, and that the happiness of self-reliance is greater than any happiness coming from dependency.

Dependent Origination

The law of cause and effect, of action and consequence, is part of the concept called Dependent Origination. Suffering is the effect of the cause of suffering; and similarly, the end of suffering is the effect of the path to the end of suffering. Dependent origination is a more detailed twelve-point description of what actually takes place in the causal process. The twelve links are ignorance; volitional formations; consciousness; mind-body; senses and sense objects; contact between sense organs, sense objects, and consciousness; feelings; craving; attachment; coming to be; birth; and old age and death. These links are said to describe a chain of causes that lead to other causes. It is important to understand that the links form a circle; there is no first link.

If one is ignorant about one's feelings of greed, hatred, emptiness, and impermanence, it indicates a lack of awareness and mindfulness. Ignorance engenders formations or fabrications—thoughts, intentions, ideas—including mental attachments and misconceptions.

The path leading to the cessation of all suffering focuses first on Right Thought and Right Intention. By cutting through ignorance, you get on the path to Right Thought and Right Intention, helping you to cut the chain of Dependent Origination.

Desire

One thing that distinguishes human beings from other animals is our interest in predicting the future. We spend a great deal of our life imagining what it would be like to be this way or that way, to do this or that, to taste or buy or experience some state or feeling or thing. By trying to exert some control over our future, we attempt to be happy.

You have your own list of "if only I had, was, could do" things. How good have you ever been at predicting the impact of attaining these things for your happiness? Did you find out that your imagination is not very accurate? Did you really feel the way you thought you would? Or did you replace that list with a whole new set of desires and cravings? It is important to see what this does to us, this always wanting more.

The question to continually ask is: "Does this want or desire or thought create well-being or does it create suffering?" When you are mindful of always wanting things to be different from the way they are, you acknowledge the cause of suffering in your life and start to end that suffering.

Disappointment

We have all faced bad news, unpleasant feelings, and true hardship. Like death and taxes, these feelings are inevitable in life. In recalling disappointments, examine in what way or ways each of these events made you wiser. We have all heard, and been inspired by, incredible stories of how people have overcome certain events in life and the lessons they have learned.

By accepting the directions your life takes, good or bad, within or outside of your control, you accept life itself. Did any of these situations help you become more tolerant of others, more patient, more content with your life? In a time of crisis or disappointment, were you able to take away a positive lesson?

Every event—trivial or life-changing, fortuitous or tragic—eventually ends. Things always change. By thinking about your former reactions to bad news, unpleasant feelings, or true hardships, you may have a delayed positive experience. Just because you did not learn something from the event when it happened does not mean you cannot learn something from it now.

Effort

Concentrate your efforts and use self-discipline to achieve the goal of Right Thought. Focusing your effort on the present, you will experience a spaciousness and ease of mind which comes from letting go of attachments.

Let your mind remain free from mental constructs, clear and vivid, effortless and undistracted. Without actively trying to block sense perceptions, imagination, recollections, and ruminations, feel that you are uninfluenced and unmoved by them as they arise. Remain at ease.

Do not allow perceptions to alter the vastness and serenity of your mind. Whenever thoughts arise, let them undo themselves as they form like a ripple in a lake smoothing out. Acknowledge emotions for what they are and allow them to pass through you like wind through the leaves of a tree. Let them be without judging or getting caught up in them. Enjoy the satisfaction that comes from this effort.

Emotional Intelligence

In his 1995 book *Emotional Intelligence*, psychologist Daniel Goleman identified five elements to emotional intelligence: self-awareness, self-regulation, motivation, empathy, and social skills. This means you understand what's going on in your head and heart; you don't make hasty decisions on impulse; you can motivate yourself to delay gratification; you listen to, understand, and relate to other people well; and you're able to focus on other people.

It's much easier to deal with emotions as they arise if you've already done a little work to create a calm inner peace through meditation.

It's not always easy to understand a feeling when it happens, especially if you think you shouldn't feel it. The best approach is to simply find the cause and effect. For example, your employer seemed unhappy with your work, so now you feel stressed; or your significant other expressed dissatisfaction, so now you feel scared. Any time you feel something uncomfortable that you'd rather avoid, look at it closely.

Once you know what you feel, you can examine the thought behind it. You can ask yourself whether you are overreacting or worrying unnecessarily. For example, maybe your manager was having a bad day and he only seemed to be unhappy with your work, or your significant other needed some emotional support that you did not give her, but now you understand and can give her this support. Then you can accept that there is an alternative—you can choose to interpret the situation a different way, soothe yourself, and then feel something different. No one else causes our feelings. Only you can choose and change them. Negative feelings are only negative if they endure because you don't let them go.

Choose to foster a sense of inner peace, challenge your perceptions and interpretations, and learn to take responsibility for your joy. You can choose to minimize your suffering and be a source of pleasure, for yourself and others.

Expectations

Each of us has a set of values and beliefs that are personal and formed by many factors. When other people do things that do not fit with your values and beliefs, you may get angry, disappointed, frustrated, or upset. You may expect other people to say or do things that you would say or do yourself. When they don't, these negative feelings that you get distract you from your potential for happiness. This is what happens when you have expectations.

Have you been upset when a loved one did not telephone you, or when you discovered that someone you care about is not as honest as you? How do you respond if a family member does not clean up after himself? What happens if someone cuts you off on the road? What happens when someone does not agree with your political or spiritual beliefs? These expectations result in your being upset. You will fare better if you find a way to let go and not let expectations create negative feelings. Respecting that others have different values and beliefs is the starting point.

You may be surprised to discover how much choice you have in letting go of expectations. There is so much to be gained by letting go of expectations and, instead, working with your values and possibilities. You will find a sense of joy and ease that is independent of the conditions and circumstances in your life.

Fear

Your fears and worries may come up quite regularly. Imagine how much energy and time you have focused on these worst-case scenarios. Imagine letting go of each and every fear and worry. Can you learn not to worry about things you cannot control, the things that might happen? Can you see how channeling your energy and time in a positive direction will make your life more fun, happy, and fulfilling?

The essential cause of our suffering and anxiety is ignorance of the nature of reality, and craving and clinging to something illusory. That is what the ego amounts to, and the fuel of ego is fear. We have our conscious day-to-day fears of an accident or health problem, for example, but there is also an undercurrent of fear lurking behind a lot of our habits. Many people even have a fear of being still.

Why do we spin out so many thoughts all the time? We sit and try to quiet the mind, but it just keeps talking. Why? It's because of this undercurrent of fear. In meditation, a lot of this becomes clear. It helps to see things as they arise, before they become full-blown and you are caught in their sway. In meditation practice you slow things down, and that allows you to see the subtle arising of fear. This helps you catch things when they are manageable. Understanding, examining, knowing, slowing down—those are the first steps in working with fear, the beginning of the path to fearlessness.

Try giving yourself a few minutes each morning to worry about your fears, then let them go the rest of the day.

Feelings Are Not Facts

It is wise to remember that, as important as feelings and emotions are, they aren't facts. Many things may produce an emotional response. Some are in the moment, others are from our past, and many are worries about the future. Other emotions may be responses to mere fantasies or even lies you tell yourself. There are a lot of positive and negative feelings that flow through your life on a daily basis. The trick is to learn how to differentiate between feelings that are born out of your imagination and thoughts and those that are based on really seeing and experiencing life.

Just because your boss or your partner looked at you in a funny way, or snapped at you, does not mean that he or she is mad at you. Sometimes people are rushed or are simply having a bad moment, and it's also possible that you are misinterpreting the message. If you create a scenario based on feelings, you can be upset for a long time by buying into those feelings as facts.

The best thing to do when you are feeling like something isn't right is to look at that feeling carefully. Don't push it down or away or try to ignore it. The only way out is by getting into the feelings and first looking at how you might be creating them.

You can combine that with some very gentle questioning of the person or people involved. Look for truth and be open to the possibility that your feelings may not be accurate. It may also be helpful to get an outside perspective from someone you trust. Acknowledging that feelings are not facts isn't easy, but it is much less painful than living your life feeling like your world is continually crashing in on you.

Friendship

To have love be part of happiness, you have to think of love beyond romantic terms and even beyond the family. Friendship love can be looked at in an almost spiritual way.

A happy life, for most people, includes genuine friendships, lasting bonds with others. It is opening our hearts to care for and about others. If we restricted our definition of love, we would be missing out on lots of ways to be happy. It would be like setting an emotional wall around you and not letting feelings enter.

Cultivate loving, compassionate thoughts about your friends. Even in the closest of friendships, there will likely be misunderstandings or even arguments. You can work to minimize that possibility or even eliminate it by practicing Right Thought and always asking yourself before you say or do something, *Is this beneficial? Is this necessary? Is this kind?* Kindness generates a spirit of friendship.

Habitual Thought Patterns

Remember that you are human, and therefore are endowed not only with habit, but also with the gift of free will. Choose to accept how things are right now, even if it's something you don't like, such as having a habitual thought pattern that is unhelpful. Say to yourself, *I am free to think this, feel this, do this, be this, experience this*, and so on.

You are free to choose a different way of thinking. You can think: *I am free to stop my habitual way of thinking, and choose what to think next.* Eliminate all-or-none thinking, overgeneralization, minimizing positive things, jumping to conclusions, blowing things out of proportion, believing that feelings are facts or reality, setting up "shoulds," taking things personally, and so on. Many of your habitual thought patterns fall into one of these areas.

Once you can recognize the thoughts, try to label them as they come up. Once you know what they are, counter each with a positive or "cooling" thought. Bring logic and rationality into those habitual thought patterns. With time you will get very good at recognizing and cooling harmful thoughts. In doing so, you will become a happier person and better problem solver.

You can break patterns of familiarity; you can change the next moment; you can do something different, something enlightened, something creative, imaginative, and fresh; something compassionate and wise.

Insight

Introspection is underrated. It is an important tool to use to put a light on in your internal life so that things are clearer when you look outward. Tuning in to your thoughts, feelings, and sensations is part of meditation. Knowing more about yourself makes it easier to deal with life and to improve your ability to care for yourself and others. Insight can make you more compassionate, kind, and loving.

Looking outward and being amidst an ever-changing world, you can be tossed around like a boat on a stormy sea. With insight and meditation, you may be able to see more clearly. Meditation focuses on the natural passing of all events within the mind and the body. The practice concentrates and calms the mind. It allows you to see through the mind's conditioning and thereby to live more fully present in the moment.

Stop from time to time during the day and pay attention to your inner dialogue. By noting that the inner dialogue is going on, you recognize that you are not your thoughts. You come to realize that you do not need to listen to and continue this inner dialogue because it gets in the way of really seeing and experiencing life in the present moment.

Practice letting go and you cultivate inner peace. Take a step toward inner peace by accepting whatever is happening in the present moment. Silently be witness to your feelings and thoughts, to sensations within your body, sights you see, and sounds you hear. Allow what is to simply be there, without wishing it to change in any way.

Mindfulness and meditation practice may indeed help you to capture and develop "flashes" of insight when they occur. The break you give your mind during these practices of introspection will allow your brain to process and integrate its ideas.

Karma

Karma means "you don't get away with nothing" (a famous quote by Buddhist teacher Ruth Dennison)—that everything you think, do, or say has an effect. This cause-and-effect connection is your responsibility. The consequence of an action, thought, or word may not instantly be evident, but it undeniably will come and there is no escaping personal responsibility for what you consciously think, do, and speak.

Understanding this is one thing, but you must constantly remind yourself. You must take the time to consider whether what you are about to do or say, or even think, is beneficial or harmful. Karma is cause and effect: what you do now, good or bad, comes back to you in the future. Your thoughts, your words, and your deeds create the experience that is your future. You need to become fully awake and conscious to all that you are and all that you can be. It is about how to purify your heart and mind by living an impeccable and enlightened life. You can help transform your existence and that of those around you.

Kindness

Everyone wants to be happy. How can we go for this in such a way that increases joy and lessens suffering in ourselves and others? How can we treat ourselves and others compassionately in trying to achieve happiness? The Dalai Lama tells everyone that his religion is kindness.

You start with being as kind as possible to yourself and then extend it to others. Just be kind, right now. No matter the circumstances, be kind. Whether it is a family member, friend, lover, someone on the street, someone who seems to hate you, or little old you, just be kind in whatever way is appropriate. The more you treat others well, the happier you feel. Kindness is the starting point, the fount from which flow so many other positive qualities such as forgiveness, generosity, honesty, and patience.

Try to remember a time when someone was kind to you, a small act of kindness or a large one. Focus on the details. Remember how appreciative you were. Remember how good you felt and how many times you told the story surrounding the event. The feeling is pretty powerful and, best of all, it is within your control.

Letting Go

It is human nature to become too attached to outcomes, things, or people. It can be very difficult to find out how to let go from these attachments even if we know that they are not good for us. The Buddha even said that our addictive behavior is the root of all suffering. But why is it so difficult to let go? Why is it so hard to give up a bad habit or an ex-lover or a negative thought?

The truth is that most of us suffer from a feeling of inner emptiness that we are trying to fill up with our various attachments—often without much success. One person may eat too much, another may cling to an unloving partner, while a third may get addicted to social media. But none of this can fill an inner emptiness.

The first step to letting go is to take a good, hard look at the things and people that we are so attached to. It is amazing how much we can deceive ourselves, believing that things and people and expected outcomes will bring us happiness when, in reality, this was never the case. Each of us needs to give up attachments and let go.

We then face the emptiness that appears when we give up a bad habit or a person who does not want to be with us. Doing this requires courage. The best practice for this is meditation—to sit comfortably and relax our whole body and mind. You will notice that the sense of craving is like a contraction in your mind that you can relax and release with every out-breath. The art of letting go is found through relaxation and love.

Love

In loving and being loved, we become most truly ourselves. Love creates true joy. In the end, nothing we do or say in this lifetime will matter as much as how much we have loved.

Become more loving and you will become more joyful. It does not matter if it is a person, an animal, or a rock. Sit by a rock and have a chat. Stroke the rock and feel at one with it. The rock may not return anything, but that is not the point of love. You become joyful because you loved that rock. And if you can do this with a rock, just think how easy it will be to move on to doing it for people and animals.

Loving- Kindness and Metta

Metta is the practice of sending out loving-kindness to strangers, associates, friends, family, and yourself. It is silently saying to yourself phrases such as these:

> May I accept this person, regardless of qualities that I do not like.

> May I be aware of this person's wish to be happy.

> May I open to this person's suffering with acceptance, compassion, and kindness.

> May the person be filled with loving-kindness.

> May the person be well.

> May the person be peaceful and at ease.

> May the person be happy physically.

> May the person be happy mentally.

As you go through the metta process, feel each phrase as vividly as possible. This is a powerful exercise because you are giving a precious gift to people and creating good karma. You are thinking of them in a positive way. You are trying to have a positive impact on their lives with nothing in return except the knowledge of your thoughts.

Meditation

Meditation is being quiet, finding a center, being in the present moment, seeking awareness and calm. Though it is spiritual, it is not necessarily "religious." You can use methods of formal meditation as well as techniques for being mindful and "awake" throughout each day.

The simplest formal meditation method is watching the breath. Sit comfortably, whatever that is for you. Let your eyes close gently. Invite your body to relax and release into the ground or cushion. Become sensitive to and listen to your breath. Breathe through your nose. Feel the air as it goes in and out of the nostrils. Feel the rising and falling of the chest and abdomen. Allow your attention to settle where you feel the breath most clearly. Focus there. Follow the breath. Allow the breath to be as it is without controlling it. Thinking will start. It is a habit. See each thought like a railroad car of a train going by. See it, acknowledge it, let it go, and come back to the breath. It does not matter how many times you get caught up in a thought or for how long. Begin again and bring awareness back to the breath. If a physical sensation or pain arises, do the same. See it, acknowledge it without getting caught up by it, let it go, and come back to the breath. For twenty minutes follow your breath with bare attention. When your mind wanders, stop and come back to the breath.

Meditation is the best tool we have to deal with thinking. Every time we let go of a thought to return to the breath we are gaining the skill we need to develop our minds. Throughout the day mindfulness allows us to catch an unskillful thought rising, and regular meditation enables us to let it go before we end up on the thinking merry-go-round.

Memory and the Future

The process of recall is actually actively constructing the past, or at least the parts of your past that you can remember. The fact that the simple act of recall changes memory means that it is relatively unstable. However, people tend to believe the opposite: that memory is relatively stable. We forget that we forgot and so we think we won't forget in the future what we now know.

When you remember your past self, it seems quite different from your present self. You know how much your personality and tastes have changed over the years. But when you look ahead, somehow you expect yourself to stay the same. We each tend to underestimate how much we will change in the future.

Our memories are highly fallible and plastic and yet we tend to subconsciously favor them over objective facts. We even think we remember what others have said. In actuality, we remember what we think others said. We make our own interpretation of the meaning and that creates the memory inside of us of what the person was saying.

This information should make you think about what you think! Don't base too much on your memory of the past, but build on lessons learned for the future.

Mindfulness

Mindfulness is attending to NOW. Being mindful calms you, and makes your mind still like a pool of water in the forest. You will see many strange and wonderful things come and go, but you will be still. This is happiness.

Look at some habits you would like to change or address. How would you like to change them? What do you see as their root or cause? If you ignore the cause, you may change the habit for a while—but it won't be a permanent change. If your habit has an effect on other people, it is important to understand the impact it has.

Bringing mindfulness to these areas is going to help. Habits are generally mindless, done on autopilot when the root or cause triggers them. One of the best mindfulness practices is slowing down or pausing when you are about to carry out your usual reaction (such as anger) or action (such as overeating). Use your determination to increase your mindfulness from moment to moment.

Monkey Mind

The mind is usually caught up in anxious thought construction and thought projection, jumping around like a monkey—from branch to branch to branch. You probably do not realize how pervasive this is in your own mind.

Close your eyes and watch the breath where it goes in and out of the nostrils. Soon a thought will arise because the mind has wandered off. Go back to the breath. When the mind wanders off again (it will!), observe what it went to—words, image, sound. Don't worry how many times the mind wanders and you have to return to focus on the breath. By learning how to focus your mind in meditation, you will slowly achieve calm and happiness.

Work toward not being carried away by monkey mind, that bunch of crazy thoughts that swing wildly back and forth in your brain, branching both logically and illogically. When you are performing a task, be right there paying attention to the details, the environment. Focus without judging these small acts. Both enjoyable and unenjoyable tasks will be completed with more efficiency and pleasure.

Morality

To cultivate Right Thought is to avoid unhealthy states of mind that give rise to suffering, such as greed or anger or hatred. This path is often called Right Aspiration and it involves actively cultivating compassionate thoughts and positive wishes for others.

The stress and unhappiness of life is caused by desires and ego-clinging. Letting go of desire and ego is the Noble Eightfold Path. The Buddhist view is that moral behavior flows naturally from mastering one's ego and desires and cultivating loving-kindness and compassion. Ethical conduct—thoughts, speech, action—is part of the path, as is mental discipline through concentration, mindfulness, and wisdom.

To be collected and controlled in our thoughts is morality. The firm establishing of the mind within that control is concentration. Knowledge within the activity in which we are engaged is wisdom. The moral quality of karma is determined by the moral quality of the motive behind our thoughts, speech, and actions.

Motives

We create karma through intentional or motivated thought, speech, and action. Constructive motives yield karmic merit and relief from suffering, while counterproductive motives yield karmic demerits and bind us further to suffering. In order to change our karma for the better, we must recondition our minds, by replacing counterproductive motives with constructive motives.

The practice of questioning motivations and intentions in daily life is very beneficial. Even questioning the small, seemingly trivial choices you make and actions you take is a helpful exercise for seeing what really drives you and creates karma.

Right Intention or Right Motive is a process of awakening. How can you see the truth of this world as it really is when your mind is clouded in unskillful intentions, motivations, desires, and ego? You can uncloud your mind by studying your intentions and watching the motives of your mind.

Our thoughts are consumed by the day-to-day activities of life. However, it is possible to form a practice of watching your intentions and asking yourself, *Why am I doing this?* or *Why am I saying this?* on a daily basis, moment by moment. The point is not to try to change your intentions, the point is to watch. Your mind will straighten itself out, one step at a time.

Maybe you can see that Right Intention is really no motive at all. Is it possible to free your mind completely in this modern age with all its complexities and detail? Maybe not, but wouldn't it be worth it to look and see for yourself? Understanding is not learned, only realized.

Negative Patterns

Even if you reframe a situation to see things differently, there will be times when you still feel negative. Sometimes negative feelings are appropriate for the events going on in our lives. Pain is part of life, and you can't avoid it by resisting it. You can only minimize it by accepting it and dealing with it well. That means feeling the pain and knowing it will pass.

You can feel whatever you feel. If you lose someone, you feel hurt. If you hurt someone, you feel guilty. If you make a mistake, you are regretful. Positive thinking can be a powerful tool for happiness, but it's more detrimental than helpful if you use it to avoid dealing with life. No feeling lasts forever.

Right Thought means sitting with discomfort and waiting before acting. Some of the most damaging decisions you can make come from feeling the need to do something with your emotions. Real power comes from realizing you don't need to act on pain. If you need to defuse negative feelings, you can channel them into something healthy and productive, such as meditation, doing something creative, or doing something physical.

Pain is sometimes an indication that you need to set boundaries, say no more often, or take better care of yourself, but sometimes it just means that it's human to hurt, and you need to let yourself go through it.

Nonviolence

The Buddha taught nonviolence, even in one's thoughts. The term *ahimsa* means "to not injure," but in the realm of thought we rarely take this into consideration. There is a belief that if we do not say or do something connected to a mean or hateful thought, it is not "out there" and we are not causing harm. That is untrue. Not only are we harming ourselves, but indirectly those mean or hateful thoughts are actually influencing our speech and actions, so we are hurting others, too.

The precept of nonviolence includes one's deeds, words, and thoughts. The essence is love. Nonviolent thought is born of awareness of suffering, both ours and others', and it is nurtured by love. Right Thought involves thoughts of selfless renunciation or detachment, thoughts of love, and thoughts of nonviolence, which are extended to all beings. Thoughts of selfless detachment, love, and nonviolence are grouped on the side of wisdom. This clearly shows that true wisdom is endowed with these noble qualities, and that all thoughts of selfish desire, ill will, hatred, and violence are the result of a lack of wisdom, whether individual, social, or political.

Overthinking

Thinking and rumination are a natural tendency and can be very compelling. You believe that if you think about something enough, you will be able to figure things out. However, at some point you can cross a line and it becomes overthinking and rumination. Overthinking causes stress and insecurity to escalate and no insight is gained. Rumination tends to make things worse.

As soon as you recognize that you are overthinking, distract yourself with an engrossing activity that is fun or happy, such as completing a crossword puzzle or hiking in the woods. The positive emotions received from distracting yourself energize you.

Another strategy for overthinking is telling yourself, *No!* or *Stop!* Or set an amount of time to do your thinking and then let it go. Yet another way is to use a journal to pour out the thoughts and ruminations, and then let them go by shutting the journal. Whatever approach you take, the important thing is that you are recognizing that you are overthinking.

Learn how to avoid future overthinking traps. If certain people, places, situations, and times trigger your overthinking—then you can avoid them or modify them enough to thwart their abilities as triggers. Learning to meditate can be one of the best things you can do to help yourself recognize and deal with overthinking and rumination. Regular meditation helps you feel less burdened, stressed, and worried. It helps you let go of anger, and forgive more easily, too.

Perception

A saying you have probably heard repeatedly is that you are what you think about all day long. Have you ever wondered why some people are happy and successful, always improving themselves, while others struggle continually and seem to spiral downward? This is what is meant by how your life is governed by your thoughts.

The difference lies in deep-rooted thought patterns, which exist in people's subconscious mind and which they think about all day. The thoughts that people cultivate and believe determine their destiny.

What are you thinking now? What were you thinking lately? Did you have thoughts of improvement, success, and abundance, or thoughts of doubt, worry, and lack? Successful people create thriving, beneficial thoughts, thoughts of self-improvement and abundance. Others focus on the times they failed and create excuses, or blame others in their minds. Subconsciously the latter are in a state of failure expectancy.

You are what you think. Don't direct your mind toward deprivation, jealousy, and what you don't have at this moment. You can choose your thoughts and focus on positive personal development. Thoughts of success and prosperity, or better personal and professional relationships, help create those circumstances. Remember, you create your life continuously through your own thoughts. Your happiness is in your own mind.

Renouncing Negative Patterns

We tend to be more reactive than responsive, which is negative and unskillful. A negative reaction starts with thought. Right Thought is taking responsibility to create your own peaceful inner world.

You can identify what you want to say yes to in life. What you want to say no to is negative patterns that come from ignorance and cause suffering. Renunciation of negative patterns is developing a perception of what makes you and those around you unhappy and then choosing not to think, say, or do those things. Renunciation is a positive and liberating process.

Renunciation is a struggle with the power of desire, attachments, and fear—but that struggle yields many benefits. You develop the inner strength to overcome temptation and compulsion. You don't have to live with the suffering and contraction that come with clinging. Clinging can be exhausting; letting go brings peace and calm and freedom.

Nonattachment, letting go of expectations in all areas of life, is cultivated through mindfulness. Mindfulness helps you to see things as they really are and to fully appreciate that negative patterns cause suffering. It helps you find the strength to renounce attachments. Mindfulness is cultivated through meditation. Use these very helpful techniques to renounce the negative patterns of your life.

Resolve

Resolve to develop a state of mind called "immovable wisdom." This means having fluidity around an unmoving center, so that your mind is clear and ready to direct its attention wherever it may be needed. No matter what the circumstance is, you will be mindful of your situation. Mindfulness is clear comprehension, paying attention to what you are doing, knowing whether actions are skillful or unskillful.

Anyone can become more fully engaged and involved in the experiences of daily life, cultivating flow. The secret is attention. What you notice and pay attention to is your experience. When you are concentrating on doing something, you are directing your attention to the task.

Examine the thoughts involved in a simple regular activity that you usually do on autopilot. Pause for a few seconds each time before you start the activity and see what those thoughts are. Then carry out the activity with gentle and complete attention and see what happens to your thoughts as the activity unfolds.

Another exercise is to sit comfortably with your eyes closed and resolve for five minutes to observe only the thought process. For these five minutes, count each thought as it arises. Your thoughts may come as picture thoughts or as words, or both together. Some thoughts may also come associated with a feeling or bodily sensation.

Let your mind be blank like a clear screen or open space and wait to count each thought, like a cat waiting by a mouse hole. After noticing and counting a thought, just wait for the next one. Do not let yourself be fooled by the thoughts. Some of them are very quiet like *It's quiet in here*, and some appear from behind like *There haven't been a lot of thoughts yet*. These are thoughts and need to be counted, too.

At the end of five minutes, most people will have seen at least five or ten thoughts and some will have counted as many as fifty or sixty. You will see what types of thoughts dominate in your mind and what kind of mental process they involve (for example, "planning" or "rehashing").

You will get a sense of how well you observe your thought process with mindfulness, noticing the arising of thought without getting lost in its story. It is a powerful and freeing realization to see that you are not your thoughts, to observe the stream of consciousness of inner thought, and to be aware of it without being identified and caught up in it.

Self

Thinking is made up of conceptualization, cognition, reasoning—mental objects. Thinking includes the recognition involved in sight, the perception that identifies physical objects. Looking at the outer world from our inner viewpoint, we are easily fooled into seeing a separate being, a "self."

The Buddha taught that "you" are not an integral, autonomous entity. The individual self, or what we might call the ego, is a delusion we experience. The central core of every being is not an unchanging self (or ego or soul), but a life current, an ever-changing stream of energy that is never the same for two consecutive seconds. The self, then, has no reality and it is only within this delusion of selfhood that suffering can exist.

When the delusion of a separate "self" is transcended and enlightenment is attained, suffering is extinguished. Part of breaking through this delusion is Right Thought or Right Intention, through which you can free your intellectual faculties from adverse emotional factors, such as sensuality, ill will, and cruelty.

With Right Intention, all of your activity becomes beneficial, whether you are cooking or cleaning or washing the dishes or driving a car or having a conversation. Everything becomes sacred because there is less fixation on the self and your intention is to generate enlightenment for the benefit of all beings.

Serving Others

The way to be happy is to make others happy. Think of ways you can expand on what you have done for others in the past. Feel the joy that comes from deeply connecting with and helping others. Your time is a gift you can offer. Everyone has the ability to give more of their time to help others achieve happiness. You have the ability to help yourself through helping others.

Thinking of others, helping others, and any other ways of getting "outside" yourself make you feel much happier. There are neuroscience studies indicating the positive benefits of getting out of our own minds. When you think and then act generously toward others, your left prefrontal lobe of the neocortex gets activated, which stimulates feelings of happiness. This floods the body with feel-good hormones and your immune functions are boosted.

Turn your focus to serving others, to what you can do to make things better all around you. Live with the philosophy of making the earth a better place than it was before you arrived.

Skillful Thoughts

Unskillful thinking is defined as thoughts that are imbued with desire, aversion, or delusion. As you may have discovered already, desire, aversion, and delusion can cause you a great deal of suffering, and can be the impetus for unkind words and actions. Hence, thoughts that are imbued with desire, aversion, or delusion are unskillful. It is important to explore just when and how frequently our thoughts are unskillful.

The Buddha doesn't just say, "Stop thinking." He suggests putting your thoughts on something else, something that can be considered skillful, a distraction of skillful nature. And having a good understanding of how obsessed people can get, how easily we get caught up on a merry-go-round of thinking, he suggests that each of us scrutinize the drawbacks of those thoughts. If your thoughts are unskillful, harmful, or result in stress—if they are imbued with desire, aversion, or delusion—then they should be abandoned. Abandoning unskillful thoughts steadies and settles the mind and concentrates it.

We all know how thinking can drag us down, yet we persist in playing these thoughts over and over in our minds. We need to look at the negative ramifications of following the unskillful thoughts, to examine how these types of thoughts have drawbacks and repercussions. This takes a bit more thinking—of the skillful kind.

Skillful thinking follows when one is mindful, present with the current task. It is imbued with harmlessness, the key word. If a thought is not causing you or others harm, it may very well fall into skillful thinking. Naturally, thoughts of compassion, generosity, and forgiveness will be skillful. But much of our lives involves thinking that is neutral, such as thinking about what to eat, what to do that day, and so on. As you become more mindful of thoughts, you will see that many of them are harmless, but that many of them can quickly lead to aversion and anger and other unskillful thoughts.

Unskillful thoughts are easiest to set aside when caught early. The practice of mindfulness will alert you as soon as you get into unskillful thoughts. Note the thought as unskillful, note the breath, then move on to something else. The Buddha is not suggesting that decision-making thoughts about problems should not occur. When he speaks of unskillful thinking, he is referring to our thinking that fosters aversion, desire, greed, hatred, and so forth—the kind of thinking that can lead to obsessions and delusions, distractions from what you really need to be addressing.

Thinking About the Past and Future

All that is certain is this very moment; the present is all that anyone ever has. So you must ask yourself: *Why do I get so wrapped up in the "what has been" and the "what will be"?* You know that your thoughts jump all over the place—making future plans, mulling over past actions, and many other forms of introspection. Often it feels like your thoughts and questions are infinite. It is not easy to be fully present in the very moment you are living. It takes strength to let go of the past and allow the unknown future to unfold itself without worry.

How can you be present when life begs you to move forward? It's in our nature to remember the past, and the future is your destination. To achieve your goals, you must plan. The choices presented to you in this very moment contribute to your power to accomplish your plan. But why get worked up about things that have yet to arise? Stressing over the future can throw you off track from your destiny. Everything happens for a reason and what will be, will be.

The best path is to not worry about the past and also not concern yourself with the future. Remember that all you have is this very moment—now.

There are so many times you are not fully engaged in your day-to-day life. Sometimes you are at work and wishing that you were home. When you are at home, you get distracted thinking about the work you have to do the next day. But if you worry about what might be, and wonder what might have been, or think you want anything to be different from what it is now, you are not in the present moment.

Being conscious of needing to be in the moment is the key to mindful living. When you find yourself thinking about the future or past, stop and take a few deep breaths to help you recenter yourself in the moment. Look at your surroundings and remind yourself to live in the present. If your mind goes to the past or future, stop yourself and bring yourself back into the moment. Appreciate the moment for what it is.

Thinking About Thinking

Reflect on the neurological turbulence underlying thoughts. Inside your own mind, try not to get wrapped up in what you think others are thinking. Getting upset about somebody else's thoughts is like getting upset about being splashed by a puddle; splashes happen! And be cautious about attributing intentions to other people. Most of the time you are just a bit player in other people's dramas; they are not targeting you in particular.

Let your thoughts about others' thoughts go. Instead, turn to practicing goodwill and generosity. Be generous and have patience. Goodwill can offer the space that you may find lacking when you are confronted with old patterns and difficult feelings, such as thinking about thinking.

Tonglen, or Giving and Taking

In order to have compassion for others, we have to have compassion for ourselves. The *tonglen* practice of giving and taking is a method for overcoming fear of suffering and for cultivating compassion. It is a method for awakening the compassion that is inherent in each of us, a method for cultivating love and compassion. It is a gentle, step-by-step process of opening the heart. By embracing rather than rejecting the unwanted and painful aspects of experience, we overcome fear and develop greater empathy for others.

Tonglen starts by taking on the suffering of a person you know to be hurting and whom you wish to help. You breathe in the wish to take away all the pain and fear of that person. Then, as you breathe out, you send the person happiness, joy, or whatever would relieve his pain.

If this is hard and you feel stuck, you can switch to doing tonglen for what you are feeling and for others who are feeling exactly the same suffering. So you breathe in for these other people and you send out relief or whatever opens up the space for yourself and those people.

Tonglen can be done for those who are ill, for those who are dying or who have just died, or for those who are in pain of any kind. It can be done either as a formal meditation practice or on the spot at any time. For example, if you are out walking and you see someone in pain—right then you can begin to breathe in their pain and breathe out relief to them.

In doing this meditation, you change the attitude of seeing yourself as more important than others. Most of us focus on our own self, thinking we are more important than others. The giving and taking practice helps you change your attitude so that you place importance on others being happy and free from suffering. You become calm and peaceful, dissolving into emptiness and the true, pure nature of the mind.

Transformation

When you discover how deeply the cause of your unhappiness is lodged in your mind, the realization comes that internal transformation is required. It is the wellspring of the spiritual quest. Self-transformation is a fundamental goal of the Buddha's teaching, an essential part of his program for liberation from suffering.

Human nature makes our thoughts tainted by anger, greed, and selfishness, our conduct fickle and impulsive, and our habits harmful and unskillful. The purpose of the Buddha's teaching is to transform us into people whose every action is pure, whose minds are calm and composed, whose wisdom has found the deepest truths, and whose conduct is always marked by a compassionate concern for others and the welfare of the world.

Self-transformation starts with an understanding of "no self" and a renunciation of clinging to an identity, the root of our suffering. We need a transformation that brings about the removal of clinging and of tendencies to self-affirmation.

In Buddhism, transforming the mind requires becoming aware of conflicting emotions, rather than pushing them away. By becoming aware of what is going on in our mind, we can learn how to deal with it. Transformation starts with meditation, paying attention to our thoughts. Buddhist meditation is designed for us to take notice of thinking.

Understanding

Understanding in Buddhism is giving up the illusion of a separate "self." There is still the body, feelings, and thoughts, but they simply are what they are—there is no longer the belief that you are your body or your feelings or your thoughts. They are exactly what they are and nothing more.

When we are ignorant, when we have not understood these truths, we tend to think things are more than what they are. We believe all kinds of things and we create all kinds of problems around the conditions that we experience. So much of human anguish and despair comes from the added extra that is born of ignorance in the moment. Everyone is influenced to do the things they do by their wrong understanding of things.

Meditation helps in understanding because you experience some tranquility, a measure of calm in which the mind has slowed down. When you look at something like a flower with a calm mind, you are looking at it as it is. When there is no grasping—nothing to desire or push away—then what you see, hear, or experience through the senses is beautiful and real. You accept the present moment, not criticizing it, not comparing it, not trying to possess or own it. You find delight and joy in the beauty around you because there is no need to make anything out of it. It is perfect exactly as it is.

Right Understanding is to be developed through reflection. When you are developing Right Understanding, you use your intelligence for reflection and contemplation of things. You also use your mindfulness and wisdom together. Use your intelligence—your ability to contemplate, reflect, and think—in a wise way rather than in a self-destructive, greedy, or hateful way.

Viewpoint

Right View supports wisdom. Wisdom in this sense is the understanding of things as they are.

Your happiness and the happiness of those around you depend on this understanding. Touching reality, knowing what is going on inside and outside of yourself, is the way to liberate yourself from the suffering that is caused by wrong perceptions. Right View is the insight you have into the reality of life, insight filling you with understanding, peace, and love.

Right View (and Right Thought) supports the other parts of the Buddha's path. Right View is penetrating insight into the nature of reality, drawing on your own observation of what happens rather than relying on the viewpoints of others. It tests intention: What did your intention lead to? What actually happened? This line of thinking teaches you to become ever more skillful.

Will

Buddhism does not suggest there is absolute free will. It teaches a middle way: that every volition is a conditioned action as a result of ignorance. So free will is inherently conditioned and not "free" to begin with. This is part of the theory of karma. Karma is primarily focused on the cause and effect of moral actions in this life. It is taught that the idea of absolute freedom of choice is unwise, because it denies the reality of one's physical needs and circumstances.

You do have choices and freedom, allowing you to make moral progress through your capacity to freely choose compassionate action. Karma means that you are responsible for your thoughts, speech, and actions, and that your afterlife is determined by the consequences of your freely chosen actions.

Words

It is important to pay attention, not just to what you say, but why, when, and how. Even the thoughts behind speech are important. By examining the thoughts and intention before you speak, you become more aware of whether what you are saying is meaningful and beneficial.

Speech is one area in which karma can be seen in an easy and direct way. Direct your attention to the state of mind that precedes talking, the motivation for your comments, responses, and observations. Try to be particularly aware of whether your speech is even subtly motivated by boredom, compassion, competitiveness, concern, fear, greed, irritation, loneliness, love, or whatever state you observe. Be aware, too, of the general mood or state of your heart and mind, and how that may be influencing your speech. Do this without judgment. Just note the motivation.

Also note the effect of your speech. What kind of response did it get? Compassion or love? Irritation or silence? With the law of karma, you have a choice in each new moment of what response your heart and mind will bring to the situation. In discovering the power of your inner states to determine outer conditions, you will be able to follow a path that can lead to genuine happiness.

You Are Not Your Thoughts

Most people believe that they are their thoughts. An awful thought enters your mind and then you think, *Wow, how could I think like that?* But you are not your thoughts. You need to understand how thoughts work so that you can change unhelpful attitudes. This is something you must experience, not just read here. By observing your thoughts, you can become aware of them without becoming caught up in them.

When you catch yourself thinking the same thought or collection of thoughts repeatedly, especially when such thoughts are affecting your mood or outlook in a negative way, this is your chance to make a positive change. You will see that your thoughts run wild like a monkey swinging from tree to tree. They run on a continuous loop when you are anxious or preoccupied, with the same thought or thoughts repeating. Stop at times and pay attention to your inner dialogue. Watch the thoughts like a tennis player watches the ball.

When you observe your thoughts, you learn how to separate yourself from them and not get embroiled in them. They are not who you are. You can become an observer, a witness to thoughts. Those anxious and emotional thoughts drive emotions: as you think so you will feel. Why feel anxious or negative or upset? Get happy by letting these thoughts go; distance yourself from thoughts that are feeding anxiety and negative emotions.

If you want to think and feel differently, meditation can greatly aid you. Remember that your thoughts are not inevitable, that they are self-made, and that they affect mood—not the other way around. By noting the inner dialogue that is going on, you recognize that there is no need to believe or continue this inner dialogue. Let it go, like a passing cloud, so you can really see and experience life in the present moment.

Meditations

MEDITATION FOR AWARENESS

Sit quietly and contemplate all the things that are going on around the earth right now. Let your thoughts calm into a deep awareness of where you are. Offer blessings or a prayer to the world. Become gently aware of the different emotions and physical and mental states of everyone out there, including animals, plants, and so on. This is awareness.

MEDITATION FOR CONFLICT

Cultivate compassion when you are having difficulty with a loved one, friend, or coworker. Sit, looking beyond the conflict, and reflect on the fact that this person is a human being like you. This person has the same desire for happiness and well-being, the same fear of suffering, the same need for love. Note how this meditation softens your feelings.

MEDITATION FOR LETTING GO OF DISTRACTIONS

Imagine that your mind is the trunk of a tree and all of your thoughts are branches. The strong branches with green leaves represent healthy mind states, while withered dying branches are distracting emotions, feelings, and thoughts. Visualize yourself reaching up to the branches of distraction and cutting them off the tree. Then let go of each distraction. You may gently label each distraction as you cut it down and let it go. Promise yourself that from now on, whenever a distraction enters your mind, you will see it, acknowledge it, then let it go.

MEDITATION FOR MIND CHATTER

Sit quietly, eyes closed, and notice each thought as it arises. Remain independent of each thought, and don't react. Simply let it go: allow it to drift out of your consciousness, just as it drifted in. Meditate like this for five to ten minutes: the benefits will be subtle but significant.

MEDITATION FOR OBSERVING THOUGHT

Count each thought as it arises—whether the thoughts are images or words or both. Let your mind be blank and wait for each thought. After noticing and counting a thought, just wait for the next one. Some of them are very subtle, so you will have to wait like a cat for a mouse. You will see after five minutes what types of thoughts dominate. This is a chance to observe the thought process with mindfulness without getting lost in each story.

MEDITATION FOR PEACE

Place a lit candle in front of you and breathe naturally, focusing your gaze on the flame. Empty your mind of all thoughts. Just gaze. Whenever the mind wanders, refocus gently but firmly on the flame. The mind can only concentrate on one thing at a time, so when you keep focused on the candle flame, you let go of what is troubling you and gain a quiet mind. Gazing at a fire in the fireplace is also calming and peaceful. If you do not have a candle handy, you can visualize one.

MEDITATION FOR PURE SEEING

Sit outside in an upright, relaxed posture. Choose a random object in front of you and look at it steadily. See it purely as a form occupying space, not naming it or judging it. Each time your mind tries to think about the object, let the thought go. Be with the act of pure seeing.

MEDITATION OF
NO- MIND

First do a twenty-minute session, standing or sitting with your eyes closed, in which you say nonsense sounds and gibberish. Use any sounds that are not actual words. You can sing, shout, mumble, whatever. In the next twenty minutes, sit still and silent and relaxed, gathering your energy. If thoughts come, be aware of them, but don't get caught up with them. Let them go. Then lie on the floor or ground for a bit, letting go even more.

MEDITATION ON DIFFICULT FEELING

Sit with a difficult feeling about some situation. Try to identify where the emotion is in your body. Pay attention to this sensation. Now gently let it go. Feel the sensation gradually dissolve. If the thought that gave rise to it remains, do not try to push it away; simply distance yourself from it. Observe it as if it did not belong to you. Allow it to fade away.

MEDITATION ON HAPPINESS

Set aside thoughts, concerns, and worries. Search in your current experience for the place inside where you feel happy or joyful. Merge with that feeling and let it permeate your whole being. Continue this as long as you can. Then open your eyes and carry this feeling with you throughout the day.

MEDITATION ON THOUGHTS

Sit and visualize your thoughts as bubbles. When you exhale, imagine all those thought bubbles floating away. Redirect your attention to your breath at your nostrils. If your mind wanders or more thoughts come, again visualize them as bubbles and let them go. Then come back to focus on the breath.

MEDITATION USING SHORT PRAYER

In any moment you can employ a short phrase or mental image to turn your mind toward grace. You can call upon this method many times during the day. You can link this conscious expression to everyday activities—washing hands, entering a new situation, beginning a snack or meal, pushing back from the desk for a break, taking a deep breath. When you link such prayers to troubling thoughts, a transformative breakthrough may occur.

MEDITATION WHEN OVERWHELMED

Take a few seconds to relax and breathe deeply. Accept that you cannot do everything at once. You can only do one thing at a time. Decide to focus on just one task and clear your mind of everything else. Whenever your mind tries to think about other things still to be done, gently bring it back to the task at hand. Now focus on that one task with mindfulness. Be aware of everything about it and use all of your senses: sight, smell, touch, and so on. Calmly watch yourself doing the task until it is done. Then move on to the next task.

MEDITATION WITH NO THOUGHT

Sit quietly and take some slow deep breaths. For five minutes, try to stop thinking. Do whatever you can to keep from generating thoughts. Do whatever works for you. At the end of the time, reflect on the experience. This exercise demonstrates that thinking cannot be stopped.

Barbara Ann Kipfer, PhD, is author of *What Would Buddha Say?* and more than sixty other books, including the best-selling *14,000 Things to Be Happy About*, as well as *The Wish List*, *Instant Karma*, *8,789 Words of Wisdom*, and *Self-Meditation*. Kipfer is a lexicographer, and has an MPhil and PhD in linguistics, a PhD in archaeology, and an MA and PhD in Buddhist studies. Visit her website at www .thingstobehappyabout.com.

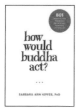
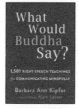